SECRETS OF
BOWDRILL SUCCESS

Fire Is Life!

Imlie

SECRETS OF BOWDRILL SUCCESS

Your Comprehensive Guide
to the Secrets and
Science Behind Rubbing
Two Sticks Together

JULIE MARTIN

FERAL HUMAN
PUBLICATIONS

The principles set forth in this book are for educational purposes.
The author, publisher and associated entities bear no responsibility
for the results of any fire making project described herein, or
for the reader's safety when doing so. Caution, common sense,
awareness of weather and a good back-up plan are always
recommended and expected when undertaking any outdoor activity.

Photographs taken by Julie Martin.
All rights reserved.

Book Design by Julie Martin

First Edition August 2016
Printed in the United States of America
ISBN-13: 978-1537015576
ISBN-10: 1537015575

Feral Human Publications
Great Meadows, NJ 08783

Contents

For Eddie:
My life would suck without you.

~ *Acknowledgments* ~

This is definitely not a book written on my own, no matter what the front cover says. First and foremost, I could never have finished this project without the love, understanding, encouragement and tolerance of my amazing partner in business and in life, Eddie Starnater. Over the past eleven years he has pushed me to succeed in everything I tried, to never give up, to never accept a lack of success as failure, to wonder, to question, to discover and most of all, to understand the secrets (he calls them "principles") behind everything that we do and every skill that we teach. He has taught me many important lessons as my main guide down the rabbit hole of Ancestral Skills, but the most important lesson he ever taught me was how to not ask questions. He taught me how to watch, observe, dissect and understand. How to find the answers on my own, and through that, how to make these skills my own. If it wasn't for his refusal to lead me by the hand down the easy trail I would never have gotten to where I am today, and would never have been able to write this book. He has been my teacher, my mentor, my guide, my love and my friend, and I can not imagine having walked this path without him.

I would also like to thank Kristy McFetridge who, although she does not know it, set an example for me that I still strive to live up to every day. During my very first days of this journey she amazed me with her skill, showed me what is possible with fire, and gave me a role model to look up to. Kristy, you are still who I want to be when I grow up, and I still remember every word of encouragement and advice you passed along to me so many years ago.

Last, to Mike Jungling, who was there to witness my very first bowdrill success on a spring evening in 2005. I'm sure he doesn't remember. I'm sure I was just one of over a hundred students and at the time I doubt he even knew my name. But Mike sat by me, encouraged, me and kept me trying "just one more time". It is because of his desire to see my success that I created the very first bowdrill coal that ultimately changed the course of my life forever. Thank you Mike!

To Stefani, who willingly and happily gave up her time and her sweat on some very hot and humid days to pose for photos; I am so grateful you have come into my life, and am so proud to be able to call you family.

To all the other teachers, friends and colleagues I have learned from and been challenged by along the way — to Seth, T-Mac, Sarah, Pfisterer, Ruth Ann, Doug, Frank, Kevin, Jorge and the many others who have inspired, taught, encouraged and cajoled me. Without knowing each of you I would never have made it this far, and I thank you all for your part in this remarkable journey.

"Don't only practice your art, but force your way into its secrets. For it and knowledge can raise men to the divine."

— *Ludwig von Beethoven*

~ *Introduction* ~

Back at the beginning of time, when the Universe came into being, all the elements came together and agreed to certain rules by which they would be bound. Rules that governed their existence, their movements, their coming and going, their interaction with each other and with every other being that did then, or ever would, be.

Since the dawn of our most ancient ancestors we have spent our lives working to find, discover, tease out and understand those Universal Laws. Today there is an entire scientific discipline devoted to discovering and understanding them. Now we call it Physics, but our ancestors simply called it Survival. If they had not figured out the physics behind the way energy traveled through rock, they could not have made tools, blades, arrow, spear and dart points; they could not have survived. If they did not figure out the physics behind the transfer of energy from one body into another through motion, they could not have invented atlatls, slings and bows. They could not have obtained food; they could not have survived. If they had not figured out the circumstances under which they could bring forth fire at will, they could not have lived through the cold nights, the changing climates or the ice ages. They would have died from exposure; they could not have survived.

In those moments at the dawn of time, Fire, creator and destroyer, bringer of both life and death, agreed to come into existence when certain conditions were met, and to disappear again when those same conditions were allowed to dissipate. Fire is a creature of balance. It cannot exist in chaos and it does not exist by chance. When the proper balance of heat, fuel and oxygen come together, fire appears. Every Single Time. It must. It has no choice. The Rules of the Universe compel it.

Today we call it "The Fire Triangle" and understanding it is absolutely fundamental to your bowdrill success. Without taking the time to develop a thorough understanding of what these Rules of Fire actually are, without respecting and honoring these Universal Laws, all your fire-making attempts will only ever be successful through luck, chance and hope. By learning how to bring together the required balance of Fuel, Heat and Oxygen, fire will reward you with its presence, Every Single Time. Throughout this book I will be stressing this point over and over and over again, because when you are making fire the Fire Triangle is the most important thing — the ONLY thing — that matters. To make a bowdrill coal, you must bring together the Fire Triangle. To blow your tinder bundle into flame, you must begin your Fire Triangle once again. To have your tinder light your fire structure, your Fire Triangle starts over for the third time.

Whether you are creating fire from sunlight, by rubbing two sticks together, hitting a piece of flint on steel or striking a modern match, the Rules of Fire *must* be followed, the required elements *must* be brought together, the necessary balance *must* be achieved, or fire is under no obligation to appear, no matter how badly you need it. Fuel, Heat, Oxygen, in balance, is all that fire needs to be your friend and companion whenever it is called.

I often wonder, with all the many, many, many ways it is possible to fail at making fire by friction, who was the first Ancestor to figure it out. Every ancient culture has its own myth or legend about how the people first got fire. There is always a time before fire, when cold and dark ruled the people's world and they were afraid. Sometimes the cold and dark were so bad that they were almost ready to die. Occasionally fire was given as a gift to help the people. In one Chinese legend a very clever young man is led by a dream to a land where he is able to figure out how to make his own fire (using the hand drill method) by watching the birds.

But by far the most common myth about the First Fire is one of theft. "Someone else" had fire who would not share it, and the people only got it for themselves through stealth, treachery or deceit. Prometheus, Loki, Mouse, Coyote, Dog, Robin, Crow and countless others all stole fire (carrying fire is how Robin got his red breast and crow his creaky voice in several diverse myths), and this allowed the people to continue to live. Where and when did these myths originate? Why are they all so similar in so many ways? Why did fire have to be stolen? Who had it? Why would they refuse to share such a life-changing, life-sustaining gift? We will never know.

What we do know is that the time before fire was a time of darkness, cold, fear and death. The ability to make fire changed our lives, changed our species, changed our world forever. The ability to make fire has made us who we are today, for better or for worse. It is our birthright, and our responsibility to carry forward the knowledge of how to make fire so that we will never know such a time of darkness ever again.

Julie Martin
July 2016

֎֎֎

"Fire Is Life."

֎֎֎֎֎

UNDERSTANDING THE PHYSICS

~ *1* ~

Understanding Bowdrill

Bowdrill fire is not that hard. It really isn't. Most people don't believe me when I first tell them that. Most people have tried and failed too many times, or watched other people try and fail too many times, or seen TV shows or Internet videos where "survival experts" exhaust themselves over and over again in order to maybe get a coal, maybe not get a coal. Or maybe they've never actually seen it done, only read about it in books and think that it is just some old "Indian trick". Some have a vague memory of trying friction fire back in their Boy or Girl Scout days, or have seen bowdrill attempted at a living history museum or powwow or Colonial Days event where the presenter explained that it used to be done "in the old days", but was not able to actually do it. Whatever their experience with bowdrill, one thing almost nobody believes is that it's really not that hard. In fact, it's actually pretty easy.

Once you have the understanding of not just how, but *why* friction fire works, once you know what your kit should look like and how it should be sized and *why* it's important to properly size your kit for *you*, once you learn how to read what your dust is telling you and *why* your dust looks the way it does, you too will be able to create a successful bowdrill coal virtually every single time.

That's right, I said it.

Every Single Time.

There are an awful lot of people out there making coals using a bowdrill kit, and there are an awful lot of videos on the internet where people will show you (or at least try to show you) how they make fire using a bowdrill kit, and there are an *awful* lot of shows on television where wilderness and survival experts will tell you how awesome they are at making friction fire, and that they've been doing it for years and that they never fail, and then proceed to work and work and work and try and try and try, and sometimes they get a coal and sometimes they don't. If making a bowdrill coal is hit-and-miss for all these "experts", then how can *you* be expected to have consistent success?

I'm going to tell you a secret. Almost every one of them is working way too hard, using way too much energy and has way too little understanding of not just what they are doing, but *why*. That is the crucial difference between someone trying to make a bowdrill coal and someone *actually* making a bowdrill coal consistently. It is the *why* that is crucial to making bowdrill almost effortless, and getting success virtually every single time.

As anyone who understands bowdrill will tell you, there is so much misinformation and poor information and downright *wrong* information out there when it comes to making fire using a bowdrill, it sometimes amazes me that anyone finds success at all. For many people I know, before they began to understand why bowdrill worked, or didn't, they felt like getting a coal was nothing but luck. That if the fire gods were smiling on them it would work, and if they had done something to offend, it wouldn't. That getting coal was, basically, purely accidental.

And the truth is, they were exactly right. If you don't know both how friction fire works and *why* friction fire works, then every time you get a coal with your bowdrill kit, it's nothing but a happy accident. I have heard many self-described "experts" say that bowdrill is not predictable. That bowdrill is difficult. That bowdrill, in fact all friction fire, is only effective maybe 30-40% of the time and really can't be counted on. I have had students tell me that they were told by other teachers that bowdrill takes a lot of strength and stamina and conditioning. That only the strongest could ever do it so they might as well not even bother trying because it would be impossible for them anyway. Honestly! These people call themselves *experts!*

I am here to tell you right now that all of that is pure nonsense. Bowdrill IS predictable. Bowdrill is NOT difficult. Bowdrill does NOT require you to have a lot of upper body strength, or stamina, or conditioning. And do you really think, do you honestly believe that if bowdrill, if friction fire in general, was only 30-40% effective, that any of us would be here right now? Our ancient ancestors' ability to make fire is what made us who we are today. If they couldn't make fire when and where they needed it they would not have survived the cold, could not have cooked their food, their brains would not have grown and we would be an entirely different species than we evolved to be.

So let's get something straight right up front. Fire is not magic. Fire is definitely magical, but it is not magic. The truth is, fire is physics. Fire is governed by the Laws of the Universe, just like everything else. If you put all the right conditions together, fire has *no choice* but to come into being. And once you understand those conditions, once you understand how to create them and how to see if and when they are in place, you will develop the amazing, beautiful and mutually beneficial relationship with fire that right now you only dream of having.

"Fire is not magic.
Fire is definitely magical, but it is not
magic."

~ 2 ~

Understanding Failure

I have always loved fire. For as long as I can remember I have been fascinated by flames. Whether they were in outdoor campfires, big ol' bonfires, our huge and ancient basement fireplace, or from the tiny candles on birthday cakes, flames and fire have always been a part of my life and a passion in my soul.

That's not to say that I was any *good* at making fire; far from it! I loved watching flames dance and change color and light up the night and the tops of cakes, but I was always one of those people who needed a whole newspaper and a can of lighter fluid to get a fire going, then spent the entire evening playing ring-around-the-rosie with the smoke. I always thought that was just how it had to be; that I didn't "get" fire and never would. I was young, and it simply didn't occur to me that I could learn a better way. Of course, I knew people who could build great fires and they assured me there was nothing to it. When I was a teenager I even learned how to maintain campfires pretty well, but getting a fire going was something I could just never get the knack of doing.

Now, I realize that it was simply because I did not understand how fire worked. No one ever taught me the science, the physics, behind fire. It was always just a bunch of wood and paper, mixed with a dash of luck, happy accident and "magic".

Not any more.

A little over a decade ago I began a whole new life-journey with fire. I had my first exposure to both building a fire structure and to making fire-by-friction during a week long class at a wilderness survival school in California, and from that moment on I was hooked.

We had to carve our own bowdrill kits out of a piece of cedar fence post and even though I had very little experience using a knife or carving wood, I worked diligently at carving my kit and was determined to make each piece as perfect as I could. Once I had my kit as perfect as my limited understanding would allow, I practiced and practiced and practiced and eventually succeeded in making a coal. Once I got home I met with only marginal success. After a while I could get a coal most times, but it was hard work! And when it *didn't* work, I had no idea why. What was I doing differently the times the coal somehow magically appeared as opposed to the times when all I got was smoke, or nothing at all?

I spent the next year practicing bowdrill, sometimes making fires and sometimes making smoke. I was not getting any better or any more consistently successful, and I was almost always exhausted and winded by the end. I didn't question it. I always just assumed, like you probably do, that bowdrill was hard and took a lot of work and was really mostly luck.

That is until one day, after watching me demonstrate bowdrill a couple of times to some passers-by at an event where we had our Practical Primitive "traveling road show" set up, when Eddie asked me, why was I working so hard? Well, I said, because this was Fire-by-Friction. You HAD to work hard! In typical Eddie fashion he cocked his head, said "Really? Huh." and walked away.

Knowing he is one to rarely give away his secrets in words, I began to watch carefully every time he was anywhere near a friction fire. I noticed that he never seemed to work as hard as I did. I noticed that he spent a lot of time working on his kit every time before he used it. I noticed that he *never* got winded and he *always* got a fire. But how? Was it just because he was Eddie, and he could do pretty much everything? Or was this something that anyone could do? That anyone could learn?

So I watched, and I practiced, and I listened to Eddie's suggestions and comments and ideas and slowly but surely I poked and prodded and figured out the science and the secrets of bowdrill. I experimented and watched and listened to fire and I challenged myself to get to know fire, to understand fire, to become a part of fire and to have fire become a part of me.

Along the way I realized that most of what I had been taught and read and seen wasn't necessarily true. I began to discover that fire itself would tell me what it needed, if I would simply pay attention to it. Over time I came to discover that yes, bowdrill fire — in fact all fire — is easy, it *is* consistent and it is something that everyone can do and anyone can learn.

Now, eleven years later, I can make a fire in the sun, wind, wet or cold. I can keep a fire going with little to no smoke, and in the rain or snow. I can make a coal and start a fire using a bowdrill kit virtually every time, using less than a quarter of the time, effort and energy of most of the people you see on TV.

And let me tell you, it feels great! The relationship I have built with fire is one of mutual respect and understanding. I know what fire needs, and by providing those conditions, fire is happy to appear and stays with me, dancing and bright and warm and amazing, for as long as I need it to be there. Then, as I let those conditions change and subside, fire slides slowly back down into the ashes until the next time we are ready to work together again.

Please don't think I am telling you those things because I am trying to brag or expound on how amazing I am or that I think myself to be some sort of "fire-making goddess". Far from it! I am telling you so that you can begin to believe that you can learn all this, do all this, be consistent and confident with all this too, no matter how much trouble you currently have making fire, or even if you've never been successful or ever even tried to make fire using bowdrill. Anyone can. Everyone can. If I can do it, so can you. It's just a matter of taking the time to understand the how and the why, putting forth the effort to practice, and having the patience and the willingness to let fire teach you.

Before I understood the physics of fire, and of bowdrill in particular, I spent a lot of time just getting smoke. And I do mean a *lot*. Usually in front of the most people possible. Of course, back in those early days, everyone who heard that I "could" make fire by rubbing two sticks together wanted to see me do it. I found myself making excuses not to demonstrate because I was so afraid of failing in front of people. I wanted to succeed so badly, yet making a coal was a crap shoot at best and an embarrassing humiliation at worst.

During the autumn of 2005, about six months after my first bowdrill success, I was, I admit it, trying to show off and demonstrate for my Dad how I could make fire using a bowdrill. He sat there patiently watching as I struggled and fussed and bowed and worked, all the while trying to avoid making too much smoke. You see, it was raining outside so I was attempting to make fire in the office of the housing development he ran and I didn't want to set off the smoke detectors and sprinklers. Yes, that is correct. I was trying to make fire, while trying not to make any smoke.

I think you can probably guess how spectacularly I failed. In front of my Dad, and several other people who had gathered to see what was going on. Great. Of course, I blamed it on the rain and the cold and anything else I could think of. But the truth was I had no idea why on earth it hadn't worked. No idea what I had done wrong. No idea that my attempt to minimize the amount of smoke I created also minimized any possibility of making fire. I was completely embarrassed, and it took months for me to let go of my humiliation, recover my confidence, and pluck up the courage to be able to pick up my bowdrill kit and give it a try once again.

Through almost three years of my failures, my frustrations, my hit-and-miss bowdrill coals, I kept holding on to one simple idea. There *had* to be a better way! Were we modern humans just not capable of reproducing the results of our ancient ancestors? If they could do it, why couldn't I? After so much time achieving only intermittent success I was determined to figure out what I was missing. To find the pieces of the puzzle that would turn my exhausting, frustrating, will-I-or-won't-I bowdrill attempts into the consistent and predictable method of fire-making that I knew in my bones it could be. That I knew it *should* be. After all, others could do it, so why couldn't I?

That was back in 2008 and Eddie and I had started Practical Primitive the previous year. I was nowhere near experienced or proficient enough yet to teach with him, but I so very much wanted to get there! I was determined to one day become more than just an intern in my own company. Since fire was my "gateway drug" into the world of Primitive Skills (the skill about which I was most passionate) I desperately wanted to find out the secrets behind friction fire, and learn to share them with others.

I knew it could be done because I had seen Eddie, and a few other primitive skills instructors that I admired, achieve the consistent and predictable results I wanted. One of the first things I noticed was that, unlike most other people I saw doing bowdrill at other schools and demonstrations and on this amazing new website called "YouTube™", Eddie didn't always just start, then work himself to death until he either got a coal or gave it up. He would check his kit before starting, make adjustments, work a little, look at his dust, work some more, make adjustments, then a minute or two later, bam. Coal. Every time.

I knew he had found this better way. I knew he was showing me everything I needed to know. I knew that, if I could find the right questions to ask, I could be as successful and consistent as Eddie. I also knew that he wasn't going to just hand it to me. I was going to have to work, try, fail, ask just the right questions, and find my own way to success.

In March of 2009 we were in Texas working with our *World of the Hunter-Gatherer* tribe (a six month skills intensive where we take a group of four individuals and turn them into a skilled and successful Hunter-Gatherer tribe). We were a couple of months into the program and they were making their first bowdrill kits entirely from materials gathered off of the landscape. One of the tribe-members, Nate, had carved his kit and was trying and trying and trying to get a coal, but all he was getting was smoke. I was watching closely to see if I could discern what the problem was; why fire wasn't showing up. When Nate took a break to rest he asked me if I had any suggestions. I told him honestly that I really wasn't sure what the problem was, but asked if it would be all right if I gave it a go. With his permission, I got myself into position and started bowing, slowly at first, trying to get the feel of this new kit. I had no idea what kind of wood I was working with (neither did Nate) so I couldn't fall back on any preconceived notions of how it "should" act or what it was "supposed" to do. Instead I had to pay attention to the wood, feel the friction and watch the dust.

Nate's bowdrill kit.

It was a beautiful, warm, sunny, Texas spring day. I could feel the heat on my back and on my neck, I could hear the *swish swish swish* as the spindle spun back and forth in the hole. I could feel the friction between the two pieces as they moved, and I noticed, for the very first time, how, as the feel of the friction changed, so did the amount of dust being generated. I was so busy paying attention to the kit and noticing what was happening with the dust that I forgot all about speed. My rhythm was slow and steady. I wasn't just on auto-pilot, pressing down as hard as possible and bowing as fast as I could. I was involved with the *process*, not the result. I was paying attention and making adjustments and watching and listening, and just a few short minutes later, bam! A coal!

Using a kit I had never touched before, with no idea what sort of wood I was using, paying no attention to speed, I made a coal. And it wasn't even that hard! That coal came to life faster and easier and with less effort than almost any other coal I had made in my life. I looked up and saw Eddie give me a slight smile and nod. I knew I was on to something.

Over the next couple of months I put what I had learned with Nate's kit in Texas into practice with my own kits at home. I went slow, watched my dust, paid attention to how it *felt*, rather than just setting to work bowing as fast as I possibly could. With a hint here and a suggestion there, Eddie guided me toward understanding not just *that* bowdrill worked, but *how* and *why* it worked. And, the times when all I got was smoke, why it didn't work. My success rate and my confidence skyrocketed, while the amount of effort and energy I was using dropped drastically. I was a woman on fire.

However, as anyone who has spent time working with fire will know, she is a fickle mistress and does not suffer arrogance lightly. As soon as you think "I've got this", fire will take a vacation and leave you hanging. Usually in front of as many people as possible!

By the summer of 2009 I had become extremely confident in my ability to make fire with bowdrill. Some might have said that I was a tad over-confident. That July we had been invited to bring our Practical Primitive "traveling road show" to a traditional archery shoot being hosted by one of the local clubs. As usual on weekends we already had workshops scheduled, but because it was for a local audience we decided I would go and run the booth at the event and Eddie would handle the workshops on his own.

The weekend rolled around and it was HOT and it was HUMID. Saturday morning I headed off to the archery club and set up our booth. I handed out brochures and chatted with lots of people and passed out schedules and answered lots of questions, and sweated and sweated and sweated in the crazy heat and humidity.

One of the questions we always get asked when folks see the bowdrill kits sitting on our table is "does that really work?", and this weekend was no exception. Less than an hour into the event a husband and wife stopped and asked if it was really possible to do bowdrill. Of course! It's easy! Would you like me to show you? It will only take a couple of minutes! I grabbed the kit, got myself situated on the ground, started going through my explanation of how bowdrill worked, and started making smoke. And dust. And more smoke. And more dust.... Where was my coal?

Finally, the couple took pity on me as I knelt there with sweat pouring down my face and dripping off my nose. They thanked me for showing them, said they "got the basic idea", and went on their way. Oh my. What had happened? Where had I gone wrong? Where was my coal?

I checked my kit and fixed up the end of my spindle and even started a new hole and carved a new notch for good measure. It must have been just a fluke.

Did I mention it was incredibly hot and humid that day?

A few minutes later a group of friends happened past. "Sure I can show you. It's easy!"

Second fail.

Third demo... third fail.

Fourth demo... well, you get the picture.

By the time lunch rolled around I had failed to make a bowdrill coal in front of at least 20 people, and I had absolutely no idea why. In addition to embarrassing myself over and over in front of multiple potential students, I was being watched closely by Jerry, who was in the booth next to mine. Coincidentally, Jerry had been in the booth right behind ours at another event just a few weeks previous. He had seen both Eddie & I do bowdrill over and over that weekend, so he knew it *could* be done and he knew that I could do it. As the crowds thinned over lunch Jerry brought out the bowdrill kit he had been working with since that last event, and asked me to help him get a coal.

Seriously? I couldn't make a coal to save my life today and he wanted me to help him get one?

"Sure", I said more confidently than I felt. "Let's see what you've got."

While Jerry worked at getting his own coal I was pulled away by another request for a demonstration, this time from a young family. I got down on one knee and mentally prepared myself to fail yet again. But this time fate intervened and I made myself a little discovery.

About half way through my talk and demo I was just about exhausted from the heat and humidity so I took a little break to wipe the sweat off my face. The little boy was curious about the kit so I let him touch the spindle. Ouch! He pulled his hand back quickly at the heat. I smiled at his surprise then touched the end of the spindle myself. Ouch was right! That spindle was HOT! Much hotter than I had ever noticed it being before. I checked the hole and it was incredibly hot as well. Now obviously, in order to make fire you have to generate heat, but this seemed more than a little excessive!

I looked down at the dust in my notch and realized that it wasn't actually dust, it looked more like chunks, or coffee grounds. After taking it into the shade under our canopy, I could see that this "not dust" wasn't that perfect dark, chocolate brown color either. It was most definitely black. I looked over at what Jerry was creating in his bowdrill notch and saw the same thing.

Suddenly, pieces started to click together in my brain.

As I believe I may have mentioned once or twice, this was all happening on an extremely hot and excessively humid day. It was about 98°F and 95% humidity; by far the hottest day I had ever worked with a bowdrill kit. It had never before occurred to me to factor in what sort of effect the external forces of temperature and humidity could have on making friction fire, but affect them they do. As I stood there sweating away on that hot and humid day, I began to realize that I was not the only thing being adversely affected by the temperature and ambient humidity. Both the fire board and the spindle were being affected as well! And because I had not been taking that extra ambient heat into account, I was not providing the proper conditions for fire to appear. I was making fire the way I always made it, without making allowances for the extra degrees and the extra moisture that already existed within the wood pieces before I ever picked them up.

My brain began to pick up speed as I worked the problem and worked my kit. I stopped doing demos and began doing bowdrill. I stopped having any expectation of success and instead began a new dialogue with fire, seeing what it had to teach me in this new place, in these new circumstances, on this particular day. Instead of being a teacher of others, I humbled myself to learn from fire as a student yet again. I started involving myself in the process, the same way I had done back in Texas so many months before. I started listening to the sounds and feeling for the friction and looking at the dust I was producing, and realizing that what was happening that day was very different from how it usually looked and sounded and felt. As my brain sped up, my bow slowed down. As my bow slowed down, my dust built up, (actual dust this time, not black chunks) and finally, after bowing much slower, and for almost twice as much time as I was used to taking, bam, there was the coal that had been eluding me all day.

The Fire Triangle

As soon as I started "taking the temperature" of my kit I realized that the harder I worked, the faster I worked, the longer I worked, the hotter my kit became. Now you might be sitting there thinking, *"you're making fire, so heat is a good thing!"* but you would be only partly correct. Heat *IS* vital to making fire, but only when it is in the correct *balance*. In order for fire to appear, three things must occur in perfect balance: Heat, Oxygen and Fuel. This is often referred to as "The Fire Triangle", and the physics of fire tell us that if any one of those three factors are out of balance in any way, fire is under no obligation to appear, no matter how hard you may work.

We have a saying at Practical Primitive: *"Where there's smoke, there's smoke."* Just because you have smoke pouring out from your fire board doesn't mean you have a coal. Smoke is *an* indicator, yes, but it is not the be-all and end-all of fire indicators.

A huge turning point in my understanding of making fire — both blowing up a tinder bundle and lighting a fire structure — was the day I learned that smoke is *incomplete combustion*. The thicker and more yellow-looking your smoke is, the closer you are to fire. However, that saying still holds true when you are creating a coal. Where there's smoke, there's smoke.

When working to create a coal using a bowdrill, or any other friction fire method for that matter, an understanding of the Fire Triangle is key. You are working to create something fragile out of a very delicate balance of factors, and if any one is off by just a little bit, you will fail in your objective. Remember, the fire triangle tells us that we need heat, fuel and oxygen **in the correct balance**.

When making a bowdrill coal, the friction between your spindle and your fireboard creates dust. That is your fuel. By pressing down hard enough on your spindle, you make that friction even more intense, which makes the dust hot. That is your heat. The notch in the hole on your fireboard is the space for all of the hot fuel to collect, and by having it the correct size of 45 degrees, you are allowing the exact right amount of air to access that hot, dusty fuel. That is your oxygen. By being conscious of creating that perfect balance and putting all of the correct factors into play every single time, you too can create fire using a bowdrill virtually every single time you try.

But how do you know you are, in fact, getting all of that right? Where do all these elements come from and how do you know they are there, let alone in balance? Throughout the rest of this book we are going to break it all down so you have a complete and thorough understanding of how and why friction fire creates a coal, and even more important, why it sometimes doesn't.

There are four major components to your bowdrill kit — bow, handhold, fireboard and spindle — and if you want to be successful with bowdrill virtually every time, you must understand the purpose and importance of them all. Ensuring that each of these pieces is the proper size and proportion for your body will immediately bring you closer to consistent, predictable bowdrill success.

There are a few other extremely important pieces that go into making your perfect bowdrill kit which too often don't get enough attention — your notch, coal catcher and tinder bundle. Every piece of your bowdrill kit is just as important as any other, and if one piece is out of whack then your entire kit will be working against you.

Most people don't understand (or at best, grossly underestimate) the importance of having a bowdrill kit that is sized appropriately for YOU. *Your* kit must fit *your* body, or you will always be working harder than you need to, and your results will always be inconsistent and based on "luck". My bowdrill kit is sized

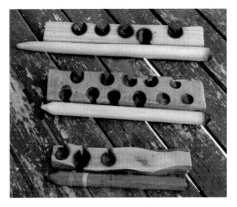

Three different bowdrill kits with three different sized spindles, belonging to three different people.

differently than Eddie's bowdrill kit, which is sized different from his daughter Stefani's bowdrill kit. The more experienced you become at making fire with bowdrill, the more you will be able to expand the sizes that will work for you, because you will understand when, where and how to compensate for pieces that are larger or smaller than would be in your perfect kit. But to begin with, you should always be working with a kit that is the right size for you.

Let's begin by looking at each piece of your bowdrill kit in turn, and learning how to figure out just what your "Goldilocks zone" (not too big, not too small, just right) is going to be. We're going to talk about each one of these bowdrill kit components in detail, because each one plays its own vital role in ensuring your bowdrill success, Every Single Time.

15

ᵔᵔᵔ

"I stopped doing demos and started doing bowdrill. I stopped having any expectation of success and instead began a new dialogue with fire, seeing what it had to teach me in this new place, in these new circumstances, on this particular day."

ᵔᵔᵔᵔᵔ

Understanding Your Bowdrill Kit

~ 3 ~

Choosing Your Bow

As the saying goes, "any old stick will make a bow". However, when you are choosing the stick that will be *your* bow, you will want to keep in mind some very important properties that will make that stick the right one for you. First, remember that both the length, diameter and weight of your bow are vitally important. Second, it is always easier to prepare a stick that is green (freshly cut from a live branch) than it is to work with a stick that has been long dead. Let's first begin with figuring out how long to make your bow.

Bow Length

For almost everyone, a stick that is about the length from your armpit to where your fingers meet your palm is just 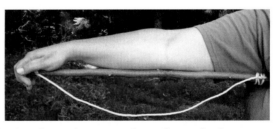 about ideal. You will often hear the "armpit to fingertips" mantra for bowdrill bows, but it has been my experience that for many people that is just a little bit too long. If you can bend your fingers down to cup over the end of your bow-stick, you will find that to be just about right. If you have to choose, having your bow a little too short is better than having it be too long.

19

We'll talk more about why that matters a little later when we get into the section on actually *using* your bow to make fire.

One thing that doesn't matter is whether the bow is curved or straight. For whatever reason — I suppose because it's  called a "bow" and a strung bow has a "C" curve to it — people seem to think that their bowdrill bow must be curved in that same manner. Not true. In fact, I prefer to use a bow that is straight, or with only a very slight amount of curve to it. A straight bow is actually easier to use than a curved bow and you will probably find that your bowing technique becomes much cleaner and more controlled when using a straight, or almost straight, bow.

Bow Diameter

What does matter — and it matters a lot — is the diameter/weight of your bow. If your bow-stick is too thick it will quickly become too unwieldy to use properly, and if it is too heavy you will find that the tip of your bow will begin to fall toward the ground as you are bowing, causing your string to go all over the place on your spindle. The stick you choose for your bow should be closer to the diameter of your thumb (bottom stick) than to, say, a broomstick (top stick). It must be large enough in diameter that it won't break apart when you split the end for your string, but not so big that it will cause trouble when you begin to  bow. A stick of about ¾- to 1-inch in diameter is usually just about ideal. However, because not all types of wood are the same weight (hardwoods such as oak and hickory are heavier than softer woods like poplar and willow) two sticks of equal length and diameter can be very different in their weight. When choosing the right bow for you, weight is just as important a factor as length.

Bow Weight

An easy way to ensure that the weight of your chosen stick will not be too heavy is to grasp your stick at one end and, keeping it at about waist height and a few inches in front of your body, hold it so the stick is straight out, parallel to the ground, for one minute. If you can easily keep the stick held out parallel to the ground for a sixty second count, you're good. If you have difficulty keeping the bow straight, or see that the tip of the bow wants to drop toward the ground, find a lighter stick. Trust me, you will thank yourself later.

Bowstring – Nylon or Natural?

If you are like most people I've met, you are keen to make your bowdrill kit as "natural" as possible as quickly as possible. One of the first places many people seem to want to "go natural" is with their bowstring. On this point, I'm going to caution you to take a step back and slow down.

We always start people out with nylon string, and transition the entire rest of their kit to "off the landscape" first. Moving to natural cordage is always the very last step of transitioning to an all-off-the-landscape kit, and there are a couple of reasons we encourage people to do it that way.

One of the main reasons we caution waiting to use natural cordage is that virtually every type of natural cordage is going to behave differently, and your method and your results will vary greatly depending on what natural material you are using, and how well your string is made.

The second reason is that most people are not as good at finding appropriate natural cordage bowdrill material as they think they are. To make a bowdrill cord is not the time to harvest a swath of dogbane, process it out and make a beautiful, double-reverse-wrap 3-foot long string that takes you hours to make, and will last one, maybe two, three if you're very lucky, attempts before it snaps. (Dogbane, like many natural cordage options, is great under tension, but it does not handle abrasion well at all.) Your bowdrill kit is the place for what we call *quicky cordage*. The twisted inner bark from a poplar, cedar, mulberry or hickory tree (hickory inner-bark makes *great* bowdrill cord!), twisted outer

Twisted Hickory Bark Cord

bark from a length of wisteria vine, braided rootlets from some bittersweet vine or a pine, spruce or fir tree are just a few examples of fast and durable options for good, strong natural bowdrill cord. Barks and roots must be kept moist in order to be flexible, but they will last far longer than many fully-processed, reverse-wrapped cords made from most common cordage plants. However, each one will behave differently from the next, and if not prepared correctly they will fail or break faster than you can make them. While natural bowdrill cords can be reverse-wrapped, simply twisting or braiding is often as (or even more) effective, depending on the material you are using.

In order to get the best results, natural cordage sometimes requires you to make changes to how your bow is strung, and use different techniques from the manner in which bowdrill is traditionally taught, depending on what type of cord you are using. Some natural materials, such as twisted

Multiple Wrap

buckskin or rawhide, can be used exactly like nylon cord. However, many natural cordage materials cannot take the tension that is a necessary part of the traditionally-taught method of stringing your bowdrill bow. Many more cannot handle the abrasion generated by the cord continually rubbing upon itself as you bow back and forth. For most natural bowdrill cords you need to use either the *Tilted Bow* or *Multiple Wrap* methods of bowing, and they take some practice. (For more on these techniques see Chapter 11, *Using Natural Cordage*.) "Cordage management" becomes a big deal and if you don't have all the rest of your kit and your form already perfect, if you don't know exactly what every other part of your body and every other part of your kit needs to be doing without having to think about it, then you will struggle not just with managing your cordage, but with every aspect of your fire-making. Your odds of getting a consistent coal will, once again, go waaaay down.

When you are first starting out with your bowdrill, start simple. Take away as many variables as you can and learn what everything is supposed to feel like under ideal conditions. That includes your bowdrill string. Start out using nylon string; just the simple white braided nylon cord that you can buy at any hardware store. Look for one that is about 3/16- or ¼-inch in diameter. A little thicker is better than a little thinner; having that extra width spreads the pressure from the string over a broader surface area and adds some additional grip on to your spindle. This can help to reduce slippage and help your spindle move more easily and evenly.

Once you are getting a coal every time you set out to make one, begin transitioning your handhold, your spindle and your fireboard, one-by-one, over to "off-the-landscape" materials. Once you are getting a coal every time with your "found" kit, *then* begin the challenge of moving over to natural string. Start with using "store-bought" natural cords — cotton shoelaces, a single strand of jute, some braided cotton kitchen twine — and begin working on managing your cordage with these easily obtainable options first. (We had one student who became so proficient that he was able to get a coal using a single strand of dental floss!) Once you are feeling comfortable and have begun having success with those easily replaceable strings, then start trying some "outdoor" options such as vines, barks and spun cordage.

Even more than the type of wood your kit is made from, the cord you use on your bow is the single biggest variable in your bowdrill kit when you gather it completely off the land. Get everything else down pat first, and then you can spend the rest of your life trying every different type of natural cord you can get your hands on!

Stringing Your Bow

While it may seem fundamental, I am frequently surprised at how much difficulty some folks go through in trying to attach a cord to their bow drill bow. There are many ways to do it, and any method that works for you is great. But for those

Watch me demonstrating this method in the **No Knot Bowdrill Bow** video on our Practical Primitive YouTube™ channel at: https://www.youtube.com /watch?v=eoD1xriC92M.

of you who struggle to keep your cord attached, or are tired of tying and untying so many knots, here is a simple technique that works just as well with modern tools and nylon string as it does with stone tools and natural cordage. Best of all you don't have to remember any knots!

1. Find yourself a stick that is about thumb size in diameter and about the length of your arm, from your armpit to your fingertips (as shown here) or  from your armpit to the end of your palm, as shown earlier.

2. Cut (or make) a length of cordage that is about one and two-thirds times the length of your bow. (A little 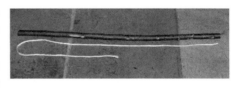 too long is better than a little too short.)

3. Hold your stick in your bowing hand (this is almost always your dominant hand), so that it is straight out from you. Does it feel easy for you to hold straight out, or does the far end feel heavy? Now hold the opposite end and ask the same questions. Whichever way feels the most comfortable — so

that the heavier end is in your hand and the lighter end is facing away from you — that is the way you should always hold your bow. It is important that you are holding the heavier end of your stick while you are bowing so that the tip will not always be dipping down toward the ground and wreaking havoc with the movement of your bowstring.

4. Decide which will be the "inside" of your bow (the side your string and spindle will be on). If your bow has any sort of natural curve, that will be the "inside". If you are using a straight stick, check if there is one way of holding it that feels the most comfortable in your hand.

5. Place your stick so that the heavy (holding) end is sitting down on something solid and the lighter (tip) end is straight up. Place your knife on the end of your stick so that it is sitting cross-wise, facing what you have decided will be the "inside" of your bow. Carefully split the tip end of your stick to a depth of about one inch. (On most people that is about the length of the middle bone of the index finger, between the two knuckles.)

6. Work one end of your piece of cordage down into the split, leaving about an inch of cordage facing the outside-side of the bow. (If the cord is too tight to fit, expand the opening by either lengthening the split by approximately another half-

inch, or by carving the top of the split into a narrow "V" groove.)

String through split.

7. Wrap your cord around the stick, passing your wrap BELOW the cordage inside the split. This will prevent the cordage from being able to slide down any further. Go around the bow a full one and one-half turns, so the long end of your cord finishes on the **same** side of your bow as the short tail. Keep this wrap tight, or the split will lengthen and your cord will get loose.

Wrap string around and UNDER tail.

Wrap 1-1/2 times until string and tail are on SAME side.

8. Pass the cordage underneath the short tail and back through the split. The long length of cordage will now be on the **opposite** side (the inside) of the bow from the short end of the string. Tighten it down so it will not move.

Pull string through split.

Pull tight through split so string is on opposite side from tail.

Tight wrap, ending with short and long ends on opposite sides of bow.

Do same at other end, wrapping short tail instead of long string.

9. Leaving a small amount of slack in your string, move to the other end of your bow and secure it using the same "split-and-wrap" technique. Once again, pay particular attention to wrap **below** the cordage within the split, and to wrap a full one and a half times around the bow before passing your cordage back through the split.

10. Any excess cordage can now be simply wrapped around the end of the split to keep it out of your way. It will be held in place with your bow hand, and you can even pass it back through the split once more to ensure it stays secured.

11. Tension on the string can easily be adjusted by simply loosening the cordage on the "holding" end of your bow and pulling the cord tighter or looser until it is the perfect size for your spindle and no slippage occurs.

Finished bow, easy to adjust, no knots.

When you are using a new string, a new spindle, or both, you will definitely get "slippage" within a few minutes of starting to work. The tension of the string on a new spindle will cause the wood fibers to compress slightly. A new cord (whether it is nylon or natural) will begin to stretch as it is used. Both of these circumstances are totally normal, so be watching, and be ready to make adjustments to the tension of your string. As soon as your string starts to slip at all while you are bowing, stop immediately and adjust your string so that it is properly tightened. If your bow is moving and your spindle is standing still you are just wasting energy and there is no point in that!

"Even more than the type of wood your kit is made from, the cord you use on your bow is the single biggest variable in a bowdrill kit gathered completely off the land."

~ 4 ~

Finding Your Handhold

Your handhold (also sometimes called a bearing block) can be made out of almost anything. Between us, Eddie and I have bowdrill handholds made out of antler, wood, bone, stone, bark, a copper plumbing fitting, the cap of a burr oak acorn and even a glass candle holder from the dollar store. The material

your handhold is made from is not important. The *shape* and the *size* of your handhold are *VERY* important. I have seen countless people struggle with bowdrill for the simple reason that their handhold is either awkwardly uncomfortable or is just plain too big.

When choosing your handhold make sure that, no matter

what it is made from, it fits comfortably in the palm of your hand. It should not be larger than the area from the base of your hand where your palm meets your wrist, up to where your fingers and your palm meet. About three to four fingers is a good guide for sizing the width of your handhold. If your handhold is too much wider than that, it will begin to jut out beyond the base of your hand toward your wrist, or past the point where your palm meets your fingers. You will very likely find that it is awkward to hold and that your hand starts to hurt or tire quickly.

If your handhold is too long, meaning that it sticks way out on either side of your palm (and this is the

Handhold fits easily and comfortably within palm.

problem I see most often with handholds), you will very likely end up holding your handhold off-center, and all the downward pressure you are exerting will be pushing in the wrong place. This will cause your spindle to get off-balance and your entire bowdrill experience to get completely out of whack very quickly. If it is slightly wider than your palm, that's okay. But if your handhold is anything more than about an inch wider than your palm it will quickly and consistently become a problem.

Downward pressure is off-center, causing handhold to tilt.

In the center of every handhold there must be a shallow indentation, about a quarter-inch deep. It doesn't need to be too deep; just deep enough that you feel comfortable your spindle will be able to spin securely and not pop out. This indentation needs to be larger in diameter than the top of your spindle so that the spindle will be able to move freely within the hole. This is one place you **DON'T** want to have *any* friction! (Conversely, all your future spindles need to have pencil-point tops that are of a smaller diameter than the indentation in your handhold.)

If you are creating a new handhold from wood, bark or some other combustible material, you can "burn in" your handhold the same way you "burn in" a hole on your fireboard. Use the tip of your knife or a sharp stone flake to create an indentation in which your spindle can seat. Next, set your spindle into place on your fireboard, then place your handhold on top, and bow. Just like you will see between the spindle and fireboard, the

friction between the top of the spindle and your wooden handhold will cause the spindle to "drill" into the handhold and create a hole. Once the hole is deep enough, stop, and put soap or grease or some other type of lubricant in

the hole to keep it from burning in any deeper. Before you begin again, be sure to decrease the size of your pencil-point on the top of your spindle. Remember, you DON'T want any friction up here, and you don't want your spindle top rubbing against the sides of the hole in your handhold. For this reason, when I'm burning in a new handhold I like to start a brand new spindle as well. This way I can leave the pencil-top a little larger than usual for the "burn in", then take it down to its proper size once the hole is finished.

Every time (or at least almost every time), before using your bowdrill kit, add a bit of soap or grease or something slippery into the hole of your

Spindle point is smaller than handhold hole to eliminate friction.

handhold to make sure that it is properly lubricated and won't cause any unwanted friction or squeaking. You don't need much; just enough to give the hole a complete covering. Turn your handhold upside down, so the hole is facing up. Then drop a little soap or grease or fat into the hole and use the pointy top of your spindle (**NOT** the flatter end that goes into your fireboard!) to rub it around and into the hole. Then turn your handhold back over again and allow any excess to drop out. Be sure to do this *away* from your fireboard! The last thing you want is to drop soap bits or a glob of grease or fat down into your spindle hole. That does not make for good friction!

Some instructors, videos and books will tell you that you can rub the spindle along the side of your nose, or up into your hairline or behind your ear in order to lubricate it. *This is very bad advice!* As modern, 21st century humans we are, in general, *much* too clean for this method to work. After you've spent a week in the woods without bathing, you may have built up enough oil on your face and grease in your hair for this to be effective, but us regular-showering bowdrill-practicing folks are far more likely to have sweat in those places than oil or grease. Rubbing your spindle in sweaty areas will add moisture to the wood, which can cause it to swell, which will *increase* the friction between your spindle and handhold instead of eliminating it. Keep a bit of soap in your bowdrill kit and use that. It will work far better and more consistently than your face!

What if you are out in the woods or are practicing with an all-natural kit? What can you use as a lubricant "in the wild"? If you are practicing your bowdrill completely off the landscape, or if you find yourself facing an emergency that turns into an unplanned survival situation, there are many things you can use to lubricate your handhold. Animal fat, crushed fresh nuts or seeds, pitch and green grass or leaves all work well to keep your spindle moving and reduce or eliminate friction between your spindle and handhold. Experiment with different options. You will find your "go to" choice, as well as a few favorite alternate options.

No matter what you end up using, be sure to keep that handhold properly lubricated, and check it every time you start working toward a coal. Otherwise you may end up with friction where you don't want it and extra work when you don't need it.

಄಄಄

"The material your handhold is made from is not important. The shape and the size of your handhold are VERY important."

~ 5 ~

Creating Your Fireboard
(and the Importance of the Notch)

Also known as a "hearth", your fireboard is the piece of your kit that cradles your coal as it comes to life. There is no particular maximum or mandatory length that your fireboard needs to be; it can be pretty much as long as you like. However it must be *at least* twice as long as your foot is wide. Any shorter and it will be difficult to keep steady under your foot while you are using any notch except the ones at the very end of the board.

Thickness

You don't want your fireboard to be too thick, because you are going to need to fill that entire notch up with dust before a coal comes into being. If your board is two inches thick, that's a LOT of dust to generate every time you want to make a coal. Conversely, if your board is very thin — if it is, for instance just a half-inch thick — the coal will be very small and quite

Finger- or thumb-thick is a good size for your bowdrill fireboard.

34

delicate and easy to break as you move it to your tinder bundle. A good guide for the thickness of your board is your index finger. If you make your board about finger-thick (or thumb-thick if you are younger or small-boned) you won't have to work too long to fill your notch, and will create a coal that is a decent size, and that will blow up easily into flame.

Width

Here again, your thumb is a good guide. I like to make my fireboards about two thumbs wide. This way I can run holes up one side and down the other, so I don't have to make as many fireboards! It can certainly be wider, although the

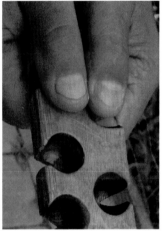

space in the middle is all just wasted, but it can't be too much narrower. In order to be

Two thumbs wide at most.

effective, your fireboard must be at least one and a half times as wide as the diameter of your spindle. If it is any narrower than that, there will not be enough mass available on the far side of the hole to keep the board together. It will very likely break, either in the middle of your

One and a half times as wide as your spindle, at least.

Holes too close mean broken boards.

hole or between two holes, and you will end up making another one anyway, so you might as well just make one that is a little wider to begin with!

Starting a New Hole

Starting a new hole in your fireboard is a great opportunity to test your downward pressure, as well as how the ambient weather conditions (heat, cold, damp, humidity, etc.) are affecting your kit.

The first hole in your board should be placed about two fingers from the end. (If you have large hands, one thumb is sufficient.) If you place it too much closer to the end you run the risk of not having enough mass on the end which may cause the board to break and "blow out" your hole. Subsequent holes should be placed at least a finger-width apart for the same reason. Your hole must also be set back from the edge of the board by about one-eighth of an inch. If you have a tendency to lean backward like I do, meaning your spindle will slide forward as you are bowing, place your hole a little farther back — three-sixteenths to one-quarter of an inch from the edge.

Set your spindle with the flatter end (the end that will be drilling into the board) in the spot you want your hole to be located and press down hard. This will create a small divot in your board. Using the tip of your knife, or a stone flake, gouge out a small hole where the divot was. This will give your spindle a place to "seat" and turn in place to begin so it won't wander on your board.

Get yourself set up in proper form (See Chapter 12), place your spindle in the gouge and begin to bow slowly, using the appropriate amount of downward pressure. You should soon begin to see smoke swirling around the base of your spindle and dust piling up around it. After a minute or so, stop and lift your spindle. There should be a dark brown circle that is at least slightly indented where your spindle was turning. If that circle is the same diameter as your spindle, you are done. If the circle is smaller than your spindle, re-set and continue bowing until the circle reaches the full size of your spindle diameter. Cut your notch as directed below and you are ready to go!

Carving Your Notch

Here we come to the most important part of your fireboard. The notch is the second most important part of that whole "physics" thing when it comes to making your fire (the most important being your spindle). If your notch is too big, too small, too shallow, or too deep into your fireboard, your chances of making a coal consistently and effortlessly will go way down.

Ideally, you want your notch to be **45 degrees** (the size of a 1/8th slice of pie) and have it positioned so the point is **just before the center** of your hole. This is pretty much the perfect size and placement for your bowdrill notch. Anything else will make consistent success just that much harder to achieve.

Notch too deep; allows tip of spindle to drill into dust pile.

If your notch is too large, or too deep into your fireboard, your spindle is far more likely to slip out of the hole, often taking your fireboard and dust/pre-coal with it. If your notch is too small, or if it's too shallow (too close to the edge of your board), the dust won't have anywhere to go. It won't be able to reach the notch so will

Notch too wide; allows spindle to easily pop out.

Notch too shallow or narrow; dust can't fall into notch.

Notch off-center; dust can't fall into notch.

37

build up around the outside of your spindle instead of falling into the notch to make your coal; the same if your notch is off-center from your hole. I can not stress enough how, by making your notch the right size and putting it in the correct place on your board, you will dramatically increase your consistency of creating a coal. Correct size and placement means more than you can imagine!

Watch Eddie demonstrate how to carve a perfect notch every time, in the *Perfect Bowdrill Notch* video on our Practical Primitive YouTube™ channel: https://www.youtube.com /watch?v=jcE3VRp1jZ4

When you are first learning, carving notches can be very frustrating; especially if you don't have a lot of experience using a knife. Believe me, I know! For years I found every excuse in the book to get Eddie to carve my notches for me whenever I could convince him to do it. But keep at it. Learning to carve your notch correctly takes practice, but is SO important to your success. Thankfully, Eddie has developed a simple way to carve a perfect notch every time and I am gong to share it with you now. It will change your notch-carving world! At least, it sure did mine.

How to Carve a Perfect Bowdrill Notch Every Time

1. A perfect notch is just about the size of a 1/8 pie slice. There are 360 degrees in a circle, so 1/8 is an angle of 45 degrees, and this is pretty much the perfect-sized angle for your notch. It must also have smooth sides, be cleanly carved, and needs to run almost (but not quite) to the center of your burned-in socket hole.

2. Once you have burned-in your socket to the full diameter of your spindle, (see page 36 for instructions on *Starting a New Hole*) take anything that has a square corner and is pliable enough to bend easily (such as a piece of paper or a dollar bill) and fold it on the diagonal. Voila! Your template for a perfect 45 degree angle! If you are out in the woods and don't have anything with a square corner, simply take anything that will fold, such as a green leaf, and fold it in half so you have a straight line. Now fold it in half again, along that  straight line, and you will have a square corner. Last, hold it with the corner facing up and fold it in half again, and you have a perfect 45 degree primitive template! Lay your template on your fireboard with the point of your template just before the center of the burned-in hole.

3. Mark an outline of the template perimeter by pressing down with your knife along both sides of your template to score a 45° V-shape into the top of your fireboard.

4. Use your knife again to mark straight down the front of your fireboard, where the scored "V" from your template meets the front corner of your board.

5. Begin removing wood from within the notch by simply *pressing* down with your knife on the CORNER of your fireboard, **not** on the flat front or the top. Just press, don't try to "carve" or saw. As you press down, keep your blade angled in at 45 degrees so that it matches the outline made with your template. Rock your knife back and forth as you press. The sharp blade edge will press down through the wood fibers and the resultant cut will be at an angle sloping toward the center of the notch along your 45 degree line.

Press and rock along template lines, first one side then the other, on the top corner.

6. Repeat the same "press and rock" from step 5 on the opposite template line, also following the inward angle. Once you have made this second cut, leave your knife in the wood and turn the blade edge toward the first cut to "flip out" the

center portion of wood between the two cuts. This will easily remove a large chunk of wood from between your two lines. **ALWAYS keep the hand that is holding the fireboard well away from where you are cutting!**

Flip out loosened wood between two press cuts.

7. Turn your fireboard upside down and repeat Steps 5 and 6 on the *underside* corners of your fireboard. Remember to press and rock your knife into the wood, don't try to cut, saw or carve it.

8. Having removed a chunk of wood from both the top and bottom corners of your fireboard, repeat these same steps on the flat front; pressing and rocking, NOT sawing or carving, the knife into the wood. Now that the top and bottom corners have been removed, you will have a much easier time removing this much smaller and more easily manageable amount of remaining wood in the center.

9. Return again to the top corner, pushing your knife into one side first, then the opposite side, again removing the resulting loosened chunk. Do the same again on the bottom corner, and again in the middle. Repeat these steps as necessary, always working the corners first, until you reach the point of your 45 degree angle that you made with your template.

10. Remove any excess material along the sides of the notch until they go straight down, perpendicular to the top of your fireboard. Make the sides as smooth as possible, cleaning up any remaining rough areas where dust may be able to catch. Be sure to check the size of your notch by re-fitting your template, and remove any additional material as needed.

If you have difficulty rocking your knife, try to hold the knife steady and rock the board instead. That works just as well. Whether you rock your knife or the board, by pressing your knife into the wood and flipping it out, you will make a cleaner V-shaped notch than by trying to carve into wood. I have seen many people try to carve out their notch and end up with a "U" that is either way too narrow or far too wide, instead of the 45 degree "V" that will bring consistent success. This technique takes practice and a sharp knife, but if you take some time to work on it, you will find that your notches begin to come quickly and easily, always the correct size and proper shape.

Finished notch; perfectly placed and sized to template.

Now I'll admit, I found it to be more than a little frustrating when Eddie first got me started using this method. I had a hard time getting the hang of just pressing into the wood and rocking my knife (or the board) back and forth, rather than sawing at it or carving down into the wood. I see the same difficulty with students all the time. Everyone (including me) wants to "carve" their notch! But when I was a "carver" my notches always ended up too wide, off-center and never quite symmetrical. In other words, I carved very poor notches that factored straight into my very poor bowdrill results. Since I started using this "press & rock" method of making my notches, they quickly became perfectly-sized, properly-placed, and I was able to make them faster than with my old carving method. My perfect notches also helped my success and consistency to skyrocket. Believe me, it may seem a little strange at first, but practicing this technique is definitely worth the initial effort!

You will probably see, or have probably seen, some people talk about "undercutting" their notch. This means that the notch is wider at the bottom that it is at the top. I'm not sure why this has become a "thing", but some people swear by it. Personally I have never found this style of notch to be helpful. It creates a strange pocket under the board that the dust sometimes has trouble completely filling. I have also found that the coal tends to stick more and that my results are less consistent. The undercutting also creates weak spots on the front corners that are more likely to break off while you are drilling down into the board. There is no reason you can't do this, but I have yet to find a compelling reason to go through the extra work and difficulty to create this undercut in your notch. With no clear benefit, I do not recommend using this method.

Another variant you'll see on notches is the "U" shape, as opposed to a "V". I believe that this became popularized due to the difficulty many people have carving their notches. (Once you begin using the "press and rock" method above, you will no longer have this problem.) U-shaped notches can work, but again, I have never been able to get as consistent results. Remember, fire is all about physics; the balance of heat, fuel and oxygen. The U-shaped notch does not seem to concentrate the heat into the center of the dust pile in the same way that the V-shape does and I think I can explain to you why that is. We're going to take a little side-trip here, but stay with me.

One of the failings of the traditional debris hut design is that V shape at the top of the frame, where all of your heat rises up to, sits, and concentrates. A dome-shaped shelter design is more heat efficient because the rounded frame allows the heat to dissipate and move throughout the shelter, as opposed to concentrating all in one place at the top of the framework. In your bowdrill notch, you WANT that heat to concentrate all in one place. You WANT the heat to hold together and build up and not move. The V-shaped notch provides that point of concentration where the heat from the dust will gather, focus, concentrate, and ultimately self-ignite into a beautiful little coal. The U-shaped notch, on the other hand, provides a more dissipated area that allows the heat to spread out and continue moving. Without having that area of concentrated heat it will take a longer time for the dust to reach its ignition point, and a longer time for you to get a coal. So while you can use a U-shaped notch and be successful in making a coal, both my experience and my efforts to quantify my results with science tell me that it will almost always take you longer. You will also expend more energy and not have the same consistent and almost effortless results.

So hey, it's just my opinion, but if I were you (and a few years ago, I was!) I'd spend the time and effort to learn how to make a perfect 45 degree V-shaped notch every single time.

No-notch Fireboard

After all that talk about the importance of having a perfect notch, I will say that it is possible to make a coal without one. In dry, arid, desert climates, notches are often not used at all. Instead, the coal is created within the pile of dust that builds up around the spindle (or stalk, when doing hand drill) in what is called a *ring coal*. Ring coals will sometimes happen in less arid climates, but they are far more rare, and usually happen more by accident than by design.

First hole, burned in about a half-inch deep.

There is another, still difficult but easier to practice, way that you can make a coal without carving a notch. There are times when, in spite of your best efforts and desires, you may find yourself in a situation where there is absolutely, positively no way that you *can* carve one. When making fire the ability to improvise, adapt and overcome is paramount, and having additional tools in your toolkit is always a better way to go. To that end I am going to briefly discuss one way that you can set up your fireboard so you won't need a traditional notch at all. This method of making a coal is definitely much more difficult, and it requires a great deal more practice than using a regular notch in order to become consistent. But it is a good technique to know and a good way to practice, both for the challenge and for the time when you just might need it.

This particular method of setting up your fireboard is a little different in that instead of burning in one hole, you will need to burn in two. The first hole must be burned in *at least* a half-inch deep; that's about as deep as you would burn down from making two or more coals. Then, set yourself ready

Spindle placement for second hole and second hole burned in.

to burn a second hole **overlapping** the first by about twenty percent of your spindle diameter. This second hole should be burned in side-by-side with your first one, with the one side of the new hole **over top** of one side of the original hole, breaking

into the side of that first circle. This hole should be burned in only the depth of a regular burn-in; just the full diameter of the spindle. (See page 36 for instructions on burning in a new hole.)

Once you have your two overlapping holes, carve or abrade a shallow V-groove into the shoulder where the two holes overlap,

Carve shallow groove to connect two holes.

effectively connecting them. This groove should be no more than half the depth of your first, deeper hole, and not more than one-third the width of the overlap, or your spindle will pop out.

Now set yourself up in proper position (as described in Chapter 12), place your spindle in the second, shallower hole, and begin to bow. If you have positioned your holes and groove correctly, the dust will begin to fall down into the deeper hole, collecting there. You

Dust collecting in deeper hole.

will have to work longer and harder for this coal, as the open collection hole allows the heat to dissipate rather than concentrate as it does in a regular notch. This means that you must pay particular attention to the balance of your Fire Triangle throughout the entire coal-making process. However, with practice and persistence, you will discover that you can create a coal right there in that deeper hole, without ever having to carve a notch at all.

As I said, this is not a simple way to make fire, but it is always better to have more options than fewer, and as you become more adept at making fire using a regular notch, this is a great method to begin challenging your skills!

દેત્ર દેત્ર દેત્ર

"Learning to carve your notch correctly takes practice, but is SO important to your success!"

દેત્ર દેત્ર દેત્ર દેત્ર દેત્ર

~ 6 ~

Sizing Your Spindle

Ah, the bowdrill spindle. This is undoubtedly the MOST important piece of your kit to have EXACTLY correct. It is also the most commonly messed up piece I see in people's bowdrill kits, no matter where I go. Your bowdrill spindle is the heart of your kit. If your spindle is off by even a little bit, your entire fire-making experience will go from consistent and predictable to guesswork and luck. You should spend more time choosing, making and refining your spindle than you do working on the whole rest of your kit combined. Your spindle *must* be straight, it *must* be round, it *must* be long enough and most important of all, it ***MUST*** be the appropriate diameter for *you*.

Your spindle is where the physics of friction fire really come into play. You see, what no one told me when I was learning, and what hardly anyone out there doing bowdrill even realizes, is that the diameter of your spindle is directly proportional to the amount of downward pressure required to make your dust. In other words, the fatter your spindle, the harder you have to press down on it.

In books, on videos and in survival school classes you will be told that your spindle should be about the same diameter as your thumb, and that is a good beginning guide. However, depending on your body size and type, your age, your physical strength, your level of coordination, any injuries you may have, and the type of wood your spindle is made from, that may, or may not, be the appropriate spindle diameter for you.

There are a lot of things to get right when it comes to your spindle, so let's get started and break it all down.

Spindle length

For some obscure reason, the "conventional wisdom" in the world of survival claims that you should make your bowdrill spindle a hand span long. Meaning that if you spread your fingers out as wide as you can, your bowdrill spindle should be as long as the distance between the tip of your thumb and the tip of your pinky finger. Why? Who knows? There is no rational, scientific or physical reason for that length. It just "is".

Conventional wisdom says your spindle should be a hand span long. This is too short!

Nine inches (the approximate distance between thumb and pinky on an average-sized person) is actually when I discard my spindle as too short and make a new one. Why do we teach (and practice) bowdrill here at Practical Primitive with a spindle length that is so contradictory to everyone else? As a good friend of ours once said, just because someone is in charge, doesn't mean they know what they're doing.

Let's take a closer look at that thumb-to-pinky length and see if it makes sense. With a 9-inch spindle, your body is crunched over, your back is hunched, your chest cavity is crushed down against your thigh and your ability to breathe is impaired. And that is when your spindle is at its *longest*. Every time you use your kit, your spindle gets shorter, meaning your body becomes more and more hunched, crushed and contorted. Why would you want to set yourself up for success by setting your body up for discomfort? When it comes to bowdrill, proper form (which we will discuss in detail in Chapter 12) is vital to achieving those consistent results you long for. Being hunched and crunched and not being able to breathe is not part of proper bowdrill form!

Back hunched and twisted

Chest cavity is crushed down on top of thigh, making breathing difficult

Entire body is off-balance

Downward pressure must be entirely generated using small muscles in forearm and wrist

Instead, consider what happens when you make your spindle about twice as long as "convention" dictates. When your spindle is made to be about two-thirds to three-quarters the height of your shin, your body is in a far more comfortable position. It allows you to remain more upright, keeps your chest cavity free to move (and breathe!) and makes it easy to keep your arm straight so that your entire upper body weight can be used as downward pressure, rather than trying to create it all using just your wrist and forearm. This is a much better way to work efficiently, without using up unnecessary calories.

Hand-span spindle above, proper-length spindle below.

Body Posture Using Proper-length Spindle

Upright position allows easy breathing

Back straight and aligned

Leaning on straight arm allows entire upper body to generate downward pressure

Body balanced and comfortable

To determine your proper spindle length, get down on one knee and bring your hand around in front of your knee as if you were going to work your bowdrill. Then lean forward, dropping your hand down the front of your shin, until you reach the "tipping point" where you feel your body start to transfer more weight on to your front leg. Where ever your hand is at that point, THAT is how long you should make your spindle. For most

adults of average height, that ends up being between 16 and 18 inches. Subtract a few inches for your fireboard and handhold and most spindles end up being about 12-14 inches long. For everyone, it is about three-quarters of the way between the ground and the top of the knee. By using this longer spindle you will find your body position to be more stable and the necessary amount of downward pressure much easier to create. Try it. You'll see what I mean.

Straight & Round

Now that you have your spindle at the appropriate length, we need to make sure that it is also *absolutely straight* and *round!* Too often spindles are carved using a knife, leaving them curved, pitted and misshapen. Or, if people are gathering a spindle off the landscape, they choose one that they think is "good enough" rather than spending the extra time to find one that is perfect. Yes, you will certainly spend more time initially when searching out a spindle that is perfectly straight, but the amount of time, effort and energy you will *save* when using that spindle will more than make up for it. Not to mention that your straight spindle will ensure that you get fire far more consistently!

What happens when a spindle isn't straight? Why is that so important? Does it really make that much of a difference? Short answer? Yes. Yes it does. When your spindle is crooked, when it has divots or curves or bumps or lumps or cracks, every imperfection will cause what we call "chatter" as your spindle turns. If your spindle is oval, or more triangular, or it has a flat side, or is in any way not round, the cord will not move smoothly over the wood and your spindle will never work quite right.

> ### Side Friction:
>
> When the side of your spindle is rubbing tightly against the side of the socket hole in your fireboard.

In addition, the wobble created by a spindle that is not straight will also create excessive "side friction" within the hole in your fireboard, robbing energy from each rotation. In bowdrill, all the important and necessary friction is occurring between the bottom of your spindle and the bottom of your socket. Any friction along the sides is just making things more difficult for you.

What you are ideally working for is having a spindle that will turn back and forth on your fireboard with ease. You want it to be smooth and clean as it turns, not clattery and bumpy and chattery. When your spindle wobbles it can cause you to lose control and make it easy for it to pop out of the board or handhold. Every bit of chatter you have as your spindle turns will affect the way the dust falls into the notch, which affects how quickly and easily, or even if, you will get a coal.

End Shapes

The ends of your spindle need to be the correct shape in order to work correctly and they are *not* interchangeable. The end of your spindle that will be fitted in your handhold should be tapered to a long narrow point, like the end of a pencil. The point should always be thinner than the hole in the

Top of spindle: tapered to pencil point that fits easily into handhold.

handhold into which it will be inserted so that there is no friction between the sides of the spindle and the sides of the handhold.

The end that will be turning in your fireboard must be a flattened curve, kind of like on the back of a spoon. Almost every time you use your spindle that bottom curve will either get

Bottom of spindle: Flattened curve like the back of a spoon.

Spindle bottoms that are too flat and too round, respectively. Both must be re-carved to proper curve before next use. (Note the dark coloring up the sides of the rounded spindle, indicating side friction.)

rounder (like the top of a baseball cap) or flatten out. When that happens, you will need to carve it back into that flat-curve, back-of-a-spoon shape before you begin using it again. If you allow the shape to remain too rounded you will quickly begin to get side friction, which steals energy with every turn. If you allow the shape to stay too flat your spindle will begin to wander on  the board rather than spinning back and forth in one place.

After you have re-carved the bottom of your spindle be prepared for some squeaking! Until the newly cut edges round back out again, they will make a terrible noise. Don't worry about it, that's totally normal. After a few turns to a minute (depending on how much carving away you had to do) the rough edges will smooth out and the squeaking will stop.

More About Side Friction

Side friction can also start to occur once you have drilled about halfway down into your fireboard. You'll know you are getting side friction when you see dark brown on the sides of your spindle, not just on the bottom. Your bowing may start to feel like it is getting more difficult and you may start to get squeaking even though you are exerting enough downward pressure.

Place your spindle in your hole and turn it back and forth with your fingers and you will feel the extra resistance. Side friction is important to stop and easy to fix. Using your knife, carefully carve away the top of your hole, all the way around, right out to the notch. Set your spindle back in the hole and turn it back and forth again. If it still feels difficult, angle the top of your hole further out. Once you no longer feel resistance, your side friction has been removed and you are ready to begin again.

Diameter

Spindle diameter is probably the most important thing to have perfect when it comes to getting a bowdrill coal with consistency and ease. As I said before, spindle diameter is where the physics of fire really come into play in a big way. We all know that in order to get a coal you need to have the right amount of downward pressure on your spindle so that it will create that lovely dark brown dust. What many people don't realize is that the amount of downward pressure required is NOT a constant. It is absolutely variable, and totally dependent upon both the diameter of the spindle, and the type of wood out of which that spindle is made. Remember, the fatter your spindle, the harder you have to press down, and a change of even one-eighth of an inch in diameter can make a HUGE difference!

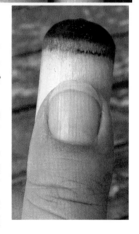

Traditional wisdom says that your spindle should be about the diameter of your thumb and while that is a good starting guide it is only that — a guide. Depending on your upper-body strength, current or previous injuries, body-type and co-ordination level, you may need a spindle that is either smaller, or larger, than the diameter of your thumb.

Even with all those factors taken into account, I have another news flash for you: ***You do not have just one spindle size!***

The *density* of the wood you are using greatly affects the amount of downward pressure you will need to exert. You can have two spindles of the exact same length and diameter, one out of hickory — a hard wood — and the other out of poplar — a medium wood — and one will work much better for you than the other. Why? The density of the wood.

If you placed your hickory spindle in one hand and your poplar spindle in the other, you would quickly notice that the hickory spindle is heavier, because hickory is a denser (harder, heavier) wood than poplar. Because of this density, the hickory spindle will require WAY more downward pressure than the poplar, even though their diameters are exactly the same.

The top spindle is made out of hickory, the bottom spindle is made out of poplar. See how the hickory spindle has a smaller diameter? I can make fire every time using the larger diameter poplar spindle (which is mine), but can not make a single fire with the smaller diameter hickory spindle (which belongs to Eddie). My hardwood spindles must be even smaller for me to be able to make a coal with ease.

When I am making fire with a poplar spindle I regularly use one that is seven-eighths of an inch in diameter. I have made hundreds of fires using that size of poplar spindle, at all times of year and under all sorts of weather conditions. But there is *no way* I can make a *single* fire using a hickory (or any hardwood) spindle of that same diameter. When using hickory, my spindle needs to be just a half-inch — over a quarter-inch smaller in diameter — in order to achieve the same results. Hard woods, medium woods and soft woods all require different spindle sizes and the only way to know for sure what size is *your* size with a given density of wood, is to give them a try.

How do you know if your spindle diameter is too big? That's easy. If you are using a good amount of downward pressure and your dust is not the color of dark chocolate, but more like milk chocolate, or closer to the color of the wood you are using, then your spindle is too big. If you are having a hard time making any dust at all, no matter how hard you press down, your spindle is too big. If you are using all your strength to press down as hard as you can in order to create the necessary dark brown dust (and are, therefore, exhausted by the time you get a coal), your spindle is too big.

When your spindle is sized correctly, creating dust that is of the proper color, and making enough dust to fill your notch and create your coal, should be relatively easy. It should NOT be an exhausting ordeal. If it is, your kit needs some adjusting and more than likely the first thing you need to do is decrease the diameter of your spindle.

So why not make every spindle the size of a pencil and then it will always be crazy easy? Unfortunately it's not that simple. Just as your spindle can be too large in diameter, it can also be too small. Most people don't realize it, but *you can overpower your spindle*. If your spindle is too small it is possible that you may press down too hard, and that can sabotage your coal just as effectively as if your spindle were too large.

When you overpower your kit you are creating *too much* downward pressure, meaning you are generating too much heat. We'll talk about this in detail in Chapter 9, *All Abut Dust*, but in short, if your dust is black, not dark brown, or if it looks like little hairs or crushed coffee grounds, you have too much heat and you need to lighten up on your pressure. While many people think that's a great problem to have, it's not always as easy to fix as you think. You can only ease up so far before you are no longer getting the necessary friction to make your dust, or your hearth and spindle begin to glaze over. Smaller spindles will also drill through the fireboard much faster than those of larger diameter because of the increase in applied downward pressure over a smaller surface. Using an appropriately-sized spindle will allow you to keep pressing down in what is a comfortable manner for you, while not overpowering your kit.

Remember, *as little as one-eighth of one inch in diameter* can make a dramatic difference in your ease of generating dust. Whatever spindle size you are using, you should find it easy and almost effortless to build your dust pile. If you feel like you're working too hard, you are working too hard! Adjust your spindle, and keep adjusting it until the amount of downward pressure is enough that you can feel it, but you can still hold a conversation and you are not exhausted or huffing and puffing by the end.

What is "Glazing Over"?

Using a spindle that is too large may cause what is called "glazing over". This happens when there is not enough downward pressure to create actual friction between the spindle and board; rather, you are polishing the surfaces instead. Polished or "glazed" surfaces will never generate dust. If you are not generating any dust and think you may have glazed over, it is easy to tell. Look into your hole and at the bottom of your spindle and see if they look shiny. Touch them and see if they feel very smooth; almost glassy. If so, you are glazed over. Before doing anything else you need to "break" your glaze.

The easiest way to do this is to take a small pinch of sand or dirt or bowdrill dust or grit of some kind and drop it into the bottom of your hole, then continue to bow. The grit grinding away between the hole and the spindle will tear up the glassiness and "break" your glaze. While it is possible to break a glaze without any grit it takes a LOT of downward pressure. Since the reason you glazed over in the first place was because you were not pressing down hard enough, the odds of you being able to break your glaze this way are slim. Even if you could, using a bit of grit is so much easier that it is almost always the way to go.

Remember, you glazed over because you were not generating enough downward pressure. After breaking your glaze, adjust your spindle size, downward pressure and form as necessary before continuing on.

"Stepping Down" Your Spindle Size

The good news is that if your spindle is too large, you don't need to find or carve an entirely new one. It is not the whole spindle that needs to be smaller, just the part that touches your fireboard. All you need to do is "step down" the bottom inch or so, and you will be good to go. "Stepping down" your spindle is quite simple. Lay your spindle on a flat, stable surface and measure about one inch up from the bottom. Set your knife down on that spot and press hard enough to make an indentation in the wood. Keeping that pressure, roll your spindle either forward or back until you have made an indented line all the way around the circumference of your spindle. Do this a few times, or until the indentation is about $1/16^{th}$ of an inch deep.

The smaller spindle on the right has been indented and is ready to be carved. The larger spindle on the left has been stepped down and is ready to use.

Move your knife to about half way between the line and the bottom of your spindle and carefully carve back up toward the indentation. Take off only small, shallow shavings. The indentation will stop your knife from going too far up your spindle, and will act as a depth guide. Once you have reached the bottom of the indentation around the entire circumference, move to the bottom of your spindle and carve carefully back up toward the section you just finished carving. Ensure that your carving is even all the way around, and that the bottom of your spindle is as circular as it was before you started. By taking away this $1/16^{th}$ all the way around you have effectively reduced your spindle size by $1/8^{th}$ of an inch and you are ready to begin again. If you need to drop your spindle size even more, repeat this process as many times as necessary until you are easily generating the soft, dark brown dust that will make your coal.

This is also an effective spindle-making technique when using "off-the-landscape" cordage that is somewhat brittle or less flexible. Making the main body of your spindle a larger size that won't require your cordage to bend tightly, while making the bottom inch the correct size for you to make a coal, will allow you to use natural cord that you would never be able to use on a spindle that was your proper diameter down the entire length.

"Your bowdrill spindle is the heart of your kit. If your spindle is off by even a little bit, your entire fire-making experience will go from consistent and predictable to guesswork and luck."

—

~ 7 ~

What About the Wood?

One of the first questions people always ask is "What about the wood? What kind of wood should I use?" Honestly, it makes very little difference. I have had people tell me that you absolutely *must* use two different kinds of wood for your spindle and your fireboard. Not true. My very first kit was cedar on cedar. I have had people tell me that you absolutely *must* use the same wood for both your spindle and your fireboard. Also not true. I regularly use a poplar on cedar kit for demonstrations. I have had people tell me that you *must* use one hard wood and one soft wood, that your spindle *must* be harder than your fireboard, and vice versa, that you *cannot* use heartwood and *must* use sapwood. I even had someone swear to me that it mattered which way the wood on your fireboard was cut — that you must *always* have the rings horizontal, never vertical. The truth is, none of that matters. That's not to say that every type of wood is going to be easy. Some woods are definitely more difficult to use than others, but when your spindle is properly sized for the type of wood you are using, many of those difficulties disappear.

So what woods are easiest? It is always best to look for a medium-hard wood like poplar, cedar, willow, tulip, etc. Look for woods that you can press your thumbnail into and leave a mark. Hard woods, i.e., hickory, oak, juniper and maple, will be noticeably heavier and you won't be able to mark them with your fingernail. They are perfectly acceptable to use, but you will need to size down your spindle, and you will work longer and harder to get them carved and shaped. Soft woods, such as basswood, are much lighter and easier to carve, but they wear down quickly and you will need to be prepared to carve a lot of notches and have an extra spindle or two ready to go.

It makes little difference if you are using wood of the same or different density for your spindle and fireboard. However, if you have one piece that is a hard wood and one that is softer, it is best to make your fireboard out of the harder wood and your spindle out of the softer. This is for purely pragmatic reasons; if your spindle is harder than your fireboard you will drill down through it much too quickly. A softer spindle will wear away faster on a harder fireboard, but you have more spindle to start out with than you do fireboard, so it just makes sense.

Woods that you'll want to stay away from, at least until you are comfortable and consistent enough to want to challenge your skills, are all the conifers (pines, spruces, firs and hemlocks) and any other resinous woods, including osage and red cedar. Woods that are high in resin can be tricky because as the wood heats up, so do the resins. Warm resins turn liquid and get very smooth, which is not at all good for creating friction, which is kind of important for creating friction fire! It is also best to avoid any toxic woods, like yew, and any types of wood that you don't want to breathe in the smoke, like ailanthus.

In the same way that resinous woods take some special skill and technique, so too do woods with pithy centers. Elderberry, for instance, makes great coals, but the pith core of the wood requires an off-center spindle that is definitely not for beginners. Stick to solid-core woods, and always go for the medium-hard wood if you can.

Just as important as the kind of wood you choose is the state of the wood itself. Remember *Fire-making Rule #1: Wet stuff doesn't burn.* The wood from which you make your bowdrill kit should be well seasoned, not green, nor should it be punky or rotting. Think "good firewood". Remember, you want it to make fire! You want it to burn! If it would make good firewood, it will make a good bowdrill kit. If it is too green or too old to make good firewood, then it will not make a good bowdrill kit either.

One last note on choosing wood: Don't fall for the idea

of the "green oak" kit. Every once in a while I'll come across a post or a video where the poster will tell people to "make a kit out of green oak and by the time the wood is seasoned enough to work, your form will be absolutely perfect!" Sometimes they'll even tell you to make a great big spindle too, just to make it particularly difficult. I can only assume this is meant as some sort of a bad joke, because it is certainly not good advice. You can practice and perfect your form using good, medium-hard, seasoned wood just as well as you can using hard green oak, and you'll actually have the fun of getting success along the way! Don't put yourself through this futility. I'll say it again, *Wet stuff doesn't burn*. And if it won't burn, it won't make fire either.

Good Woods for Practicing Bowdrill

- White Cedar
- Cottonwood
- Willow
- Aspen/Poplar
- Tulip Poplar
- Beech
- Alder
- Box Elder
- Basswood
- Birch
- Maple
- Ash
- Palm
- Mullein (dry stalk)
- Yucca (dry stalk)
- Sotol (dry stalk)

This is not by any means a comprehensive list; there are many great fire-making woods not shown here. It is meant only to give you a place to start if you are new to bowdrill and want some good options with which to begin.

Don't get too caught up in finding the *perfect* kind of wood for your kit. Remember back to Chapter 1 and my story about getting a coal using Nate's bowdrill kit down in Texas? I had no idea what kind of wood I was using for either the spindle or the fireboard. It is far more important to correctly size the pieces, to stabilize your form and to read what your dust is telling you than it is to be able to name the kinds of woods in your kit. (You'll learn all about *"Reading Your Dust"* in Chapter 9.)

Wood Pile Challenge

If you or someone you know has a wood pile, try the *"Wood Pile Challenge"*. Choose different pieces of straight-grained wood off the pile to make a fireboard and spindle. It's an easy way to get experience making fire using many different types of wood, especially hard woods, which are the most desirable for wood stoves and furnaces and therefore always likely to be found on wood piles. I have made "wood pile" kits out of black walnut, hickory, oak, birch and more.

For these "experience" kits, I will split out an appropriate-sized section then use the chop saw and belt sander to refine and shape my fireboard and spindle. The purpose of the challenge is to practice *making fire*, not building kits, so make them as perfect as you can using whatever tools you have, then give it a go. The more different types of wood you have experience using, the better your bowdrill fire-making skills will become!

ॐॐॐ

"If it would make good firewood, it will make a good bowdrill kit. If it is too green or too old to make good firewood, then it will not make a good bowdrill kit either."

~ 8 ~

Coal Catchers & Tinder Bundles

Coal Catcher

There is one more, often under-valued, piece of your kit called a "coal-catcher". This is the bit that sits underneath the notch in your fireboard, which all the lovely dark-brown dust falls down onto. When I first learned to make friction fire I was taught to put a small piece of my tinder bundle underneath my fireboard to use as my coal-catcher, and this I did for about the first year. Until I learned more about tinder. I am here to tell you all, *don't do this!* Do not use any of your tinder as your coal-catcher. Why? Good tinder is dry, hair-fine, fluffy (has lots of space for the oxygen component of the Fire Triangle) and lights easily. By shoving some of your tinder under your fire board you are putting it in direct contact with the cold, moist ground and crushing it flat. Cold, moist and crushed does not good tinder make!

Plus, those fine little threads of your bit of tinder can stick up into the notch itself, preventing the dust from compacting, coalescing and forming a

Tinder coal-catcher being pulled up into notch, obstructing dust.

coal. Or, as you drill down farther into your board, your rotating spindle may snag one of those fine threads and pull the rest of the tinder up farther into the notch, preventing any dust from falling down at all. I have seen (and experienced) so many things go wrong with this method that I will say once again, **don't do this!**

Instead, take a small piece of something that is thin and flat enough not to cause your fireboard to wobble when you place it underneath, yet strong enough to be able to hold the coal as you lift it up and into your tinder bundle. My favorite thing to use is a bit of birch bark, but I have also used other thin barks like beech, young poplar and young maple. Another good option is a strong dry leaf, like oak or tulip poplar, so long as the dry leaf is still in good condition. If it is a large leaf, fold it in half, or even quarters, to provide an extra layer of strength and stability and it will work great. If the ground

Birch bark coal-catcher, allowing dust to fall cleanly and unobstructed into notch

is very cold, set your entire kit on something thick, like a jacket or piece of bark, to provide an additional layer of insulation.

If you have a piece of thin cardboard from a box of cereal or crackers, or a bit of wrapper from a granola bar or some candy, those kinds of things can also work. You just need something that is sturdy enough to hold the coal when you pick it up to put in your tinder bundle. There is nothing worse than having a beautiful smoking coal, and when you pick it up, half-way to your tinder bundle your coal-catcher collapses and your coal breaks into pieces when it hits the ground. Sadness!

Constructing a Tinder Bundle

Tinder is dry, hair-fine material that lights easily. That last part — lights easily — is especially important. It might be dry, it might be hair-fine, but if it does not light *easily* it is not good tinder. There are all sorts of materials that make good tinder, (including store-bought jute string) and every ecosystem has different "go to" tinders. Here in our part of New Jersey, our number one go-to tinder is pine needles. Brown, dry pine needles are easy to find, take no processing and they go up like gasoline.

Another type of regularly-used tinder, both around this area and in many others, is inner bark. Below the rough, outer bark of a tree there is another layer called the "inner bark". On many trees, including cedar, poplar, hickory, some maples, basswood and many others, the inner bark is composed of many thin layers. When dry, these layers can be pulled apart into thin strips that can be buffed up into small, hair-fine strands that make an excellent tinder bundle.

Wherever you are, there will be something that can be used as tinder. Whether it is pine needles, inner bark, dry grass, dry leaves, seed heads, weed tops, birch bark, cattail down, thistle heads, wood shavings, or a pulled apart cotton ball, the common denominator remains the same: Dry, hair fine, lights easily.

> When using grasses for tinder, remember that they are hollow and can hold moisture inside that hollow core long after the outside of the grass appears dry.
> If grass does not snap when you try to break it, if you have to pull or twist or cut it, the grass is NOT dry.
>
> Just like good kindling, grass must SNAP easily in your hand to be considered good tinder.

Your tinder bundle can be made out of all one material or you can combine multiple different types of tinder together if none of them are quite perfect, or found in enough quantity. Different tinders ignite at different temperatures and burn at different rates, so a "multi-tinder" bundle can be an advantage at times. Pine needles ignite readily and have a good burn time. Dogbane fibers on the other hand, even though they are finer than pine needles, take longer to light then burn up more quickly. Ultra-fine materials like the down from cattail, thistle and milkweed, light incredibly easily, but burn up so fast that they create more of a flash than a burn. If some of the material in your bundle takes longer to light, put it near the bottom and place the easiest-to-light tinder topside and center, right where your coal is going to sit.

The actual construction of a tinder bundle is quite simple. Find a surface for processing your tinder fibers over top of so that they can be collected and saved (i.e. a table, an article of clothing, a flat rock) Wherever you are making your bundle, be sure your tinder is always kept off the ground, and is protected from both moisture and wind.

Inner bark of an Atlantic White Cedar tree: This stringy inner-bark is easy to pull apart and makes a great tinder bundle.

1. Working directly above your cleared area, shred up any larger material such as bark, down into stringy fibers.

Pull the strands off of the bark piece, then pull your inner bark apart and shred it down into stringy fibers.

2. Rub the strings between your hands to buff the fibers thoroughly, breaking the strings into softer strands, and allowing the smaller particles and dust to collect on your working area. Pull these strands apart into individual fibers, being sure to allow the smaller bits to drop onto a surface where they can be easily collected.

3. Take the largest of these buffed, softened fibers or dried grasses or whatever you have, and set them onto your fingers with your thumbs in the center. Turn the pile in a rotating circle, keeping your thumbs in the center to form an indentation. This will create a "bird's nest" that is about the size of your palm. This will

be the base layer of your tinder bundle.

4. Place your next finest, next easiest to light materials (seed heads, weed tops, etc.), as well the largest pieces of fluff that fell while you were processing your larger fibers, into the center of your bird's nest. Don't pack down your fibers as you add them. Allow air space and loft

in your bird's nest, as proper air flow is crucial for ignition. (Remember your Fire Triangle!)

5. Continue adding the finer and finer material into the center of your nest until it is all inside your bundle.

These are the finest, softest, easiest-to-light, powdery fibers. Place them in the very center of the top layer of your tinder bundle. Place your coal right on top of these fibers!

When creating in ideal tinder bundle it should look almost like a bulls-eye when finished, with smaller rings of finer materials layered on top of each other. While this level of detail is not strictly necessary, by practicing creating the best possible tinder bundle for your coal to light up you will know exactly what to do when weather conditions are against you.

No matter what materials you decide to use for your tinder, one thing is certain: a properly prepared tinder bundle can mean the difference between the warm glow of fiery success and the cold sting of having to start all over yet again. Remember that **the purpose of your tinder bundle is to light your fire**, so your bundle *must* burn long enough and hot enough to ignite the tinder and kindling within your fire structure.

Practice as much as you can with different types of tinder. Practice with large and with tiny tinder bundles. Practice using easy-to-light materials and materials that are difficult to blow into flame. Practice using tinder that is slightly damp on days it is very humid or has just rained. Go out on "tinder walks" where you search for

> Learn to build a simple fire structure that emits lots of heat, lots of light, makes great coals and requires very little maintenance in our **Log Cabin Fire Structure** video on our Practical Primitive YouTube™ channel: https://www.youtube.com/watch?v=0ZzdLmGZrf8

and harvest materials you think might make good tinder, then bring them home to try. There are plenty of tinder materials out there but they all behave differently and you need to know how to work with them *before* you really need them.

So there it is. You've got your kit perfectly sized, your spindle perfectly sized and perfectly straight, your notch perfectly cut, your tinder bundle prepared and you are ready to get started! Now what? How does one go about getting this consistent and effortless coal that I've been talking about since the beginning of this book?

"A properly prepared tinder bundle can mean the difference between the warm glow of fiery success and the cold sting of having to start all over yet again."

~ 9 ~

All About Dust

Whether it is bowdrill, hand drill, fire saw, fire plow, fire thong or something else, when it comes to making fire by friction, you live or die by your dust. If you are successful, thank your dust. If you fail, look to your dust because it will tell you everything you need to know about why you did not succeed. Learning to "read your dust" is absolutely key to being consistently successful with bowdrill because it will tell you when everything is going right, as well as when it is all going horribly, horribly wrong.

Color

The first thing to be watching for in your dust is the color. In order to create a coal you must have heat, and it is the color of your dust that tells you exactly how much heat you are creating. Your goal is to create soft, beautiful dust the color of dark chocolate. The farther

away from that color you are, the more work you have to do before you will be successful. The lighter in color that your dust is, the cooler it is. The darker your dust, the hotter it is. (And yes, it can be too hot.) If you are creating dust that is about the same color as your spindle or fireboard, or maybe just a little darker, or even the color of, say cumin or cinnamon, your dust is not hot enough to cause a coal to come into being. No matter how much of it you create, you will not get a coal with light-colored dust.

| The dust shown here is the exact same color as the fireboard. The color is far too light and it will never make a coal. | While this dust is darker, it is still closer to the color of cumin or cinnamon than it is dark chocolate. This dust is still too light. | This is the dark brown dust, the color of dark chocolate, that we are looking for. This dust is hot enough to reach the temperature required for a coal to self-ignite. |

The pile shown here has light dust through the main body, with dark brown dust on top.

Because the core of the pile is comprised of the lower temperature, light-colored dust it will not make a coal.

To get that vitally important darker dust there needs to be more friction between your spindle and fireboard, meaning you need more downward pressure (or occasionally more speed). If you are already pressing down on your spindle as hard as you *comfortably* can (in other words, you are **not** bearing down with every ounce of strength you've got, burning out your muscles and quickly becoming exhausted, but are pressing down with a reasonable amount of pressure that your muscles can comfortably hold for several minutes and you can still easily hold a conversation) then your spindle is too big around and you need to take down the diameter.

What I did not understand during those first frustrating, fail-filled years is that the amount of downward pressure required to get that dark brown dust, is directly proportional to the diameter of your spindle. In other words, the fatter your spindle, the harder you have to press down. And since you can only press down so hard, based on your physical size and condition, it is important to have a spindle that is correctly sized *to you* in order to have consistent success. For some reason I have yet to understand, many people seem to feel that dropping down to a smaller size of spindle is some sort of bad reflection on their skill, or on their worth as a human being or outdoorsperson. That is simply not true! Your bowdrill kit MUST be sized perfectly for YOU, not your friend or spouse or neighbor or instructor. Even as little as one-eighth of an inch in diameter can be the difference between simple success and frustrating failure.

If your dust is not the color of dark chocolate, you need to press down harder and get it to be that color or you will not create a coal, period. If you can not comfortably press down any harder than you already are, decrease the diameter of your spindle. It's as simple as that.

Particle Size

Just as too large a spindle can keep you from getting a coal because your dust is too light, a spindle that is *too small* can thwart your efforts just as effectively. Remember that your goal is to create beautiful, soft, fine dust the color of dark chocolate.

Just as your dust can be too light, it can also be too dark.

Working too hard and creating too much downward pressure is just as big of a problem when it comes to your all-important dark-brown dust. Too much downward pressure creates too much heat. Remember, our Fire Triangle tells us that heat, fuel and oxygen must be present *in the correct balance*. Too *much* pressure (generating too *much* heat) throws off that balance and impedes the coal-making process. Once again, your dust will tell you everything you need to know.

If you are one of the many bowdrill fire-makers out there who press down as hard as you can and bow as fast as you can for as long as you can manage it, whether you realize it or not you have probably encountered this very problem more than once. Next time, take a look in your notch and see what's there. Odds are that you are not actually creating a pile of nice fine chocolate brown dust, but instead, have in your notch what looks more like a bunch of short little hairs. This is the first indicator that you are working too hard and your kit is getting too hot, too fast. Hairs are usually created in conjunction with dust and as soon as you see them you know that you need to ease up, slow down, and get your heat back in balance with your fuel and oxygen.

If you keep going as you are, keep pressing down as hard as you can and bowing as fast as you can, instead of dust or hairs you will find yourself looking down at a pile of little black chunks that look almost like crushed coffee grounds. (We call these "platelets".) These charcoal black platelets are telling you that you are working **way** too hard and generating **far** too much heat. You really need to dial it back and ease up on how hard you are working, because your dust is telling you that you are working way too hard!

Dust is the ideal medium for making a coal. It all falls down on top if itself into a compact pile within the confined space that is your notch. All that ideally balanced amount of heat concentrates together until it gets to just the right temperature that it self-ignites into that beautiful little coal you have been working toward.

Hairs make the whole process just a little harder. They are long and thin and therefore don't compact down as well as dust does. This leaves more air space in between, throwing off that critical fuel, heat, oxygen balance. Even though the individual strands are hotter, the extra space between them means that you will likely need to work longer to generate the necessary level of heat in the center of the pile where that coal gets created. If you don't pay attention to the hairs as they arrive, you are missing an

Too much heat — usually caused by too much pressure, too much speed, or both — creates hairs instead of dust.

important cue and may or may not make a coal. If you keep going too long with too much heat, you will quickly move into the next, and least desirable state of production, platelets.

Platelets are the most difficult material from which to make a coal. Their black color tells you that you are creating a LOT of heat, but it also tells you that the amount of heat is overwhelming the fuel source and kicking your fire triangle dangerously out of balance. The fuel you are creating is simply too large for the amount of heat that is usually generated. Platelets are large, irregularly-shaped and allow a lot of extra space for air within your notch. Because of their irregular shape they really do not want to coalesce together to make that coal.

They crash down on top of each other like hail, instead of falling gently like snow.

While it is definitely possible to make a coal that contains platelets, it usually happens if you start kicking them out only near the end, and not for too long. If you started out making dust and ended up with the platelets after a time, the heavier platelets can actually crush and extinguish the fragile dust coal that is forming in the center of your notch, so be careful.

Excessive heat — caused by far too much speed or pressure, or by too much speed and pressure combined with high humidity — creates platelets instead of dust.

Composed almost entirely of hairs and platelets, this pile of overheated non-dust would not make a coal, no matter how many times the student tried to re-heat it. There was too much space within the pile and it simply would not come together into a coal.

If you do manage to get a coal made of a high proportion of platelets, your odds of being able to transfer that coal into your tinder bundle without it breaking apart are much lower than with a dust coal. You will need to let your coal sit and rest for enough time that it will coalesce together at least a little, or the whole thing will break apart on transfer.

When you see hairs or platelets on top of your fireboard, around your spindle or falling in your notch, immediately slow down, ease up and try to reverse the process back to dust.

If you see hairs or platelets falling into your notch, immediately slow your bowing and ease up on your pressure until you see the process begin to reverse and the color return to brown. If you have already built up too much heat and can't get back to dust, stop. At this point your dust is telling you that your entire kit has become far too hot and continuing to work won't do you any good; you will just be wasting energy. If you touch the bottom of your spindle you will see what I mean. (But be careful! I actually burned my leg once when I accidentally dropped my too-hot spindle!) Now touch the side of your spindle and see how high up from the bottom you can feel heat. If you have been kicking out platelets, odds are your spindle will be hot an inch, or even more, up the sides. Set everything down, discard what is in your notch, take a break for a few minutes and allow your whole kit to cool down.

Once your spindle has cooled, carve the black char off the bottom before starting again. Before you begin working toward another coal, re-assess your pressure and speed. If you can't go slower or lighter, it's time to move to a larger diameter spindle. Just like going down in diameter, as little as one-eighth of an inch can make all the difference in leaving your platelets behind and getting that much-sought-after dust into your notch.

Our final note on reading dust takes us all the way back to Chapter 5 and notch placement. Remember, if your notch is too shallow, too narrow, or off-center, the dust cannot fall down into it correctly. Your dust will tell you almost immediately when this is the case. When you are bowing, if you see that dust is building up around your spindle almost right from the start, your notch needs to be fixed. Until your notch is completely full, all the dust should be falling down into it, not building up around your spindle. The sooner you fix your notch, the sooner your dust will fall correctly and the sooner you will get your coal!

Learn to read your dust. Your dust is your best friend when it comes to friction fire and it is sitting there trying to tell you exactly what is going on in your kit and what you can adjust to make things better. Don't just practice making coals, practice making dust. Try to make hairs. Figure out what it takes for you to make platelets. Watch to see at what point your dust stops being dust and what you have to do to get it back again. When you are successful making a coal, study it for a minute before moving it over into your tinder bundle. When you are unsuccessful, study it even harder. Successes are great, but failures are what truly teach you. Look at the color, the consistency, what it is made up of — dust, hairs, platelets, or a combination of all three. The more you study your dust, the more consistently successful you will become, I promise you.

"When it comes to making fire by friction, you live or die by your dust."

~ *10* ~

Building Your Kit

"But wait," I can already hear you saying, "if I was in a survival situation I could never find pieces that long and straight and round and perfect." That may be true, but it's probably not. I have never not been able to find a proper-length spindle or a proper-sized fireboard "off-the-landscape". You will need to have a little more patience and persistence and look around a little longer to find the right size and length that you need, rather than just "making due" with the first "close enough" piece you find. A little time spent here will save a lot of time (and effort and energy and calories) down the road. As the saying goes, "the short cut is almost always the long way around." Virtually every time I say "good enough" instead of taking the time to find what I *really* need, I spend more time fussing with and fixing my kit than I ever would have just finding the right pieces in the first place.

However, it is also important to remember that what we are creating here is your IDEAL bowdrill kit. Your *PERFECT* bowdrill kit. Your *EFFORTLESS* bowdrill kit. Whether you make your kit from pieces bought at a lumber yard or from wood gathered off the landscape makes no difference. An off-the-landscape kit can be just as perfectly made and sized and prepared as one made out of dimensional lumber and dowels. So let's take a minute now to talk about making your bowdrill kit.

Lumber-yard Kit

It is very easy to make your entire bowdrill kit from pieces you buy at a lumber yard, or that you may even already have in your garage or basement. We regularly make what we call our "Home Depot Kits" for student use and for sale. They are quick, easy and inexpensive to make, and they remove all the variables, allowing you a consistent experience for your beginning bowdrill attempts.

Dowel Spindles

Poplar dowels can be found at every lumber yard and home improvement store, as well as at many hardware stores and craft-supply stores, such as Michaels and Hobby Lobby. They may be labeled as "poplar", "softwood" or just as "dowels" and are the most commonly found. You will also find oak dowels in some stores, which are a darker color and usually labeled as either "oak" or "hardwood" in order to differentiate them from the more common poplar dowels. They are available in sizes ranging from one-quarter inch all the way up to 1-1/2 inches in diameter, in eighth-inch intervals. These dowels make perfect bowdrill spindles, and because they are so inexpensive, are a great way to figure out your ideal medium-wood spindle size. Decide

Bowdrill kit made entirely from the lumber yard: Poplar dowel spindle, cedar 1x2 fireboard, red oak 1x2 handhold, poplar board bow and nylon cordage.

which size is closest to the diameter of your thumb, then purchase that size, as well as one size smaller and one size larger in diameter. Make your spindles and give each a try until you find the one that works best for you. These dowels can be easily cut to your perfect

Four poplar dowel spindles, sized 1/2, 5/8, 3/4 and 7/8 of an inch in diameter.

length, and the ends quickly carved using a sharp knife. If you have some type of belt sander, shape your ends that way; it's even faster.

Oak dowels are a great way to figure out your approximate hardwood spindle size without having to spend the time going out to find then shape a whole spindle without knowing whether or not it will be right for you.

One note about dowels, and about all lumber in general. Quality is not what it used to be. Over the past two years we have noticed a remarkable decline in the quality of wood available at most home improvement stores, and that includes dowels. Many are not straight, but either curved or s-shaped, and some would do better as hockey sticks than as bowdrill spindles. You will also find some that are still a little green (sometimes literally) instead of fully cured. I strongly recommend that you don't just grab the first dowel you pull off the rack. Bring out several dowels, look down the length to see if they look straight, then lay them on the floor of the store and roll them. If your dowel doesn't roll easily, making little noise, it is not straight. Put it aside and try another one until you find a dowel that is perfectly straight.

Cedar Fireboards

Cedar lumber is a little harder to find than it used to be, but can still be purchased at Lowes, as well as some other smaller chains and local stores. (Home Depot does not carry any cedar lumber.) Find a cedar 1x2, sometimes called "cedar furring strips". These are usually six or eight feet long and separate from the rest of the cedar boards meant for decking and other building projects, often near the back of the store or on an end cap. Again, check to see that your board is *straight*, and find one that is as knot-free as you can. I usually have to go through five or ten boards before I'll find one that is appropriate for use as a fireboard. But once you find a good piece of cedar you can get five or six fireboards out of your single purchase.

Cedar fireboard, cut from 1"x2" cedar furring strip.

Cut your board into five or six pieces and do yourself the favor of lightly sanding the corners and the cut ends; they tend to splinter and that's never fun. That's it! There's your brand new cedar fireboard. Burn in, cut your notch and get started!

Handhold

We often use the red oak "end-cuts" left over from our Board Bow workshops as handholds. They are already the perfect 1x2 size to fit well in the hand, and when cut into three-inch lengths they work great. You can buy 1x2x24" oak boards if you like, or use any other piece of wood you have lying around, left over from some other project. If you don't have any extra wood, cut off a piece of your cedar board and use that. It is not necessary that your handhold be made from hardwood. Any type of wood will do once it has been properly lubricated to not allow friction. Measure the width of your palm (or about three inches) and cut your cedar to that size. Sand all the corners and edges down into a nice comfortable curve so they won't cut into your palm, burn a hole in the center (or drill a shallow indentation using a 3/8" or ½" drill bit) and you are ready to go.

Bow

We've already talked about finding a simple bow on the landscape, and that's really the easiest way to go. However if you live in an area where you can't cut any tree branches, and won't be getting out to the woods any time soon, you can make a bow out of 1/4 x 2 inch poplar board. It usually comes in either two-foot or four-foot lengths, so you could potentially make two bows, or just have some left over.

Cut your board to your correct length (as described in Chapter 3) and if you wish, sand and round the ends. This isn't necessary for function — it just looks nicer. Measure one inch down from one of

Hole drilled in tip end of bow.

the ends (it doesn't matter which) and drill a hole in the center of the board that will be large enough for your string to pass through (3/16- or 1/4-inch). At the other end, measure down one inch and make a mark, then measure down another inch and make a second mark. Drill a hole on each mark. Cut a piece of nylon cord that is about one and two-thirds the length of your bow and tie a knot in one end. Pass the knotted cord through the **single** hole and pull until the knot is against the board. (This will be your bow tip.) Make sure the knot is large enough that it won't pull through the board.

Two holes drilled in holding end of bow.

Knotted end of string pulled through *single* hole in *tip* end of bow.

Now take the free end of your string down to the two-hole end of your bow (the end you will hold while bowing) and pass it up through the hole **closest to the end of the board.** The free end of your cord is now on the same side as the knot. Pass the string back down through the second hole so the free end is now on the opposite side of the bow as the tip-end knot.

Free end of string passing down through hole ***closest to the end*** of the bow.

Leaving a bit of slack in your string, wrap the free end around the board, between the two holes, underneath the loop of string on the knot-side, and overtop of the slack length of cord that has come down from the tip.

This wrapping secures the string

String passing back up through second hole.

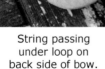

String passing under loop on back side of bow.

Wrapped back of bow.

Wrapped inside of bow. (Side the string is on.)

while making it easy to adjust to fit any spindle size without having to deal with knots. By holding your hand around the end with the wrapped cord you will help to keep the string from slipping, and keep any excess cordage out of your way.

There are some people out there who will try to tell you that making a kit this way is "cheating". That the fact your fires were created from a kit you made using materials you purchased makes them somehow "less" than someone who made their kit out of found materials. I think that's just silly. There are always going to be people out there trying to put you down for one reason or another. Don't pay any attention to them. The wood you are using is still wood, whether it was processed by you or by a lumber mill. Wood is wood. If you can make fire from it, you are amazing, no matter where that wood came from originally.

One of the reasons we prefer to use these ready-made kits to start new students is that in modern society most people do not grow up learning good knife and carving skills. Too many people give up before they start because they feel neither confident nor comfortable using a knife so their kit either never gets built, or is not flat/straight/round/true enough to work properly. Starting off with a pre-made kit that is the perfect size and is perfectly shaped isn't "cheating", it is a smart way to remove all of the variables, understand how everything works, and gain the confidence and success that will encourage and inspire you to begin working with more difficult materials.

These kits are a great beginner option, and if you are just starting out, or have been having difficulty with kits you have made, we hope you will give lumberyard kits a try. You don't have to make a whole kit this way. Try just using the dowel spindle so you can feel what a perfectly straight and round spindle is supposed to feel like. Or use the cedar board to get a feeling for a good medium-hard wood that will allow you to easily carve your notches. Whatever pieces you use to help gain understanding, confidence and success, those are the right pieces for you.

Off-the-Landscape Kit

For those of you with a little more skill or experience, or who are feeling up for more of a challenge, let's talk now about gathering a kit off the landscape.

Spindles

No matter what part of your kit you are looking for you always want to find material that is as close to your finished product as possible. The less shaping and adjusting you need to do, the better. This is probably most important when it comes to your spindle.

Every off-the-landscape spindle you make should be as perfectly straight and round as any lumber yard dowel. Found materials are no excuse for sloppy work. Keep searching until you have found a piece that is fully dry but not soft or rotting. One that is the correct length as described in Chapter 6, at least mostly round, and **straight**.

For whatever reason, that last criterion always seems to cause the most difficulty for people. We tell them to find something straight, and they come back with pieces that are curved, bent, wiggly and everything but straight. "Almost" will not work when it comes to your spindle. "Close enough" is not good enough here. In spite of what I have had students try to

Bowdrill kit made entirely off the landscape: Elderberry spindle, cedar fireboard, acorn cap handhold, autumn olive bow and twisted hickory inner bark cordage.

tell me, straight *does* occur in nature, and perfectly straight *is* perfectly possible to find. All you need is patience, and the mind-set that will not settle for less than perfect when perfection is required for your live-or-die success.

Split-timber Spindle

Spindles can be made from "in-the-round" pieces, like tree branches, or they can be split out from a larger piece of straight-grain wood. If you are going to carve your spindle from a piece of split wood, don't try to carve it round right from the start. It almost never works out as well as you plan, unless you are very talented, or very lucky!

Split out into a square.

Square taken down into an octagon.

Instead, start by splitting your wood into a square that is only slightly larger than your desired spindle diameter. Get all four sides as close to the exact same width as you can, making your future spindle as square as possible. Next, carve down all four corners of your square, so you have an octagon. Again, get each of the eight sides as close to the exact same width as you can; they should all look exactly alike. Make sure your cuts are straight and even all the way down the entire length of your spindle. Remember, straight is KEY when it comes to having a good spindle.

Now that you have a nice straight, even octagon you can actually stop here if you wish. Each side of your octagon is narrow enough that while the spindle is not a

Straight, round, split timber spindle.

perfect circle, the corners will quickly be worn down by the tension and action of the string. If you are planning on using one of the techniques for natural cordage from the next chapter, having these corners can be to your advantage, as they provide something for your string to hold onto when there is no tension on the bow.

However, if you want to take your spindle down to round, ***do not*** do any more carving! Put your knife away and instead find some sandpaper or a rough rock or patio stone or piece of concrete, and use that to *sand* the corners down until your spindle is perfectly round.

Spindle in the Round

To make a spindle "in the round", find a dry, round(ish), straight piece of branch that is a little larger than your ideal spindle size for that type of wood. If

Straight, dead cherry branch, ready to be made into a spindle.

you don't know what type of wood you are looking at, press your thumb nail into an exposed, bark-free area and see how deep it will make a mark, if at all. How easy it is to make a mark will tell you if you are harvesting a soft, medium or hard wood.

All fire kit pieces should be gathered from a fallen tree, fallen branch, or something that is standing dead; remember that it must be dry and cured, not fresh or green. Cut the piece to your appropriate length, remove any remaining bark and assess for any bug damage, soft spots or knots that may cause difficulty.

Standing dead cedar tree.

Once you have your de-barked spindle piece, carve the

De-barked and ends carved.

pencil point end for your handhold and the flattened, back-of-spoon curve that will go into your fireboard. Lay your spindle down on as flat a surface as you can find and roll it. Rolling your

spindle will immediately tell you how close to round it is, and where any high spots are that need to be fixed. Get your head down low so that you can see where the spindle and surface meet and look for any light that you can see shining through between your spindle and the flat surface on which it is sitting. The areas that touch the flat surface, on either side of the space where you can see daylight, are the spots you need to fix.

Where most people go wrong at this stage is they get out their knife and begin to carve. Stop! Put your knife away! Carving your spindle is a sure-fire way to create divots and flats spots and holes where you don't want them. If you have ever carved a spindle before I'm sure you have experienced that moment when you were working your spindle down into round, taking those final carves to get one section perfect, when your knife suddenly caught a growth ring and before you realize it you had carved off a much larger piece than you intended. Your spindle was back to flat on one side, instead of the almost round it had been a moment ago. This is how many spindles end up too crooked or too small — carving error.

Instead of carving your spindle, shape it. Use sandpaper or a rock, concrete step or anything rough to sand your spindle

Hold your spindle with two hands and move it **diagonally** across the surface you are sanding on. Working diagonally goes much faster than a straight forward or sideways movement.

into shape. In spite of what you may think, shaping and sanding your spindle this way is actually *faster* than trying to carve it down. Sand for a minute, then check and roll your spindle again. Find the high spots and sand them down. Sand, shape, check and repeat, until there are no more high spots and your spindle is straight, round, smooth, and ready to go into your string.

Spindle after being sanded; no more light shining through underneath, because the high spots have all been sanded down.

Fireboard

Probably the biggest mistake I see when people are gathering a fireboard is they start off with something that is too big. Many people's first experience making a kit came in a class where they made their whole kit out of a large wood round, like a fence post, so that is what they look for. Remember, your fireboard only needs to be a twice as long as your foot is wide, and one and a half times as wide as your spindle. For most people, that means a stick of about "OK" diameter and a hand span long will suffice. Longer is perfectly fine, but too

De-barked birch branch that is about one foot long and of "OK" diameter.

short is too difficult to keep stable under your foot when you are bowing. There is no need to hunt for large chunks of wood; a small section of tree branch will almost always be ideal. The easiest and fastest-to-construct boards are made out of straight-grain wood pieces, so always look for straight grain if you can find it. (And if you are patient and take your time when looking, you almost always can!)

Remember that, just like for your spindle, wood for your fireboard needs to be dry and well-cured, not fresh-cut or green. Remove the bark and check for any soft spots, rot or knots that may be an issue.

Take your straight-grain, hand-span long, "OK" diameter, section of branch, set your finger over the widest part of one

end and make a mark on either side. Now set your hatchet on one of the marks and split straight down along the grain to the other end. Do the same on the other mark to complete your rough-out of your fireboard. If you don't have a hatchet, you can use your knife (provided it is longer than your branch is wide). Set your knife on top of the mark and use a pounding stick to whack it into the branch to create the split. Do the same on the other mark to complete your rough-out. Set your roughed-out fireboard on a flat surface and check to see if

Your fireboard does not need to be perfectly flat, only flat enough that it won't wobble or rock under foot when you are bowing.

it lays flat or has any wobble. Use the same sanding technique you used for your spindle to flatten the bottom surface if needed, or the top of your board, if desired.

If your wood piece is not straight-grained you can use your knife or hatchet to do some roughing out, but stop before you get to your final thickness so you don't accidentally gouge your board too deep. Once you get it carved close to finger-thick, put your knife away and finish taking it down by using the sanding technique from making your spindle. Sand it down to the final finger-thickness and make sure it sits flat with no wobble. You can also sand the top of the board down closer to flat if you like; this can make it easier to carve your notch.

Finger-thick fireboard.

If you don't have any cutting tool you can sand your entire piece down in the same manner you did your spindle. This will take a while, but will definitely be effective and will probably go faster than you think.

Once your fireboard is the appropriate thickness and flat enough that it won't wobble on the ground, take a look at your front and back edges, where you will be carving your notches. If they are very curved you may want to sand them down so they are flatter and more perpendicular to the top side, but this is not always necessary. If they are only slightly curved they will probably work as-is, and you can at least give it a try before deciding whether or not to flatten them out.

Finished cherry spindle and birch fireboard, ready to be burned in.

Two-stick Fireboard

What if you can't find an appropriate "OK" diameter branch? What if you don't have a hatchet or machete or knife that is large enough to split out a fireboard and you really don't want to spend the time to sand the whole thing down? What do you do then? If you have some extra string, or can manufacture an additional 12- 18 inches of, strong, small-diameter cordage that will wrap tightly, then this is the time to employ the ***two-stick fireboard***.

Instead of a finger-thick board, the two-stick fireboard is made from two spindle-sized sticks lashed together. To make this type of fireboard, find two dry, well-cured, thumb-thick sticks of the same type of wood, preferably the same type as your spindle. Cut or break them to the same length as you would a

Two dry, de-barked sticks cut to length.

regular fireboard; twice the width of your foot, or about a hand span, long. (You can also make your board from two old spindles that have gotten too short for use.)

Now hold your two sticks side-by-side and tie a half-hitch or a timber-hitch around one of the sticks, about an inch from the end. Tightly wrap your cordage three to five times around the two sticks together. Then slide your string between the long ends of the two sticks, bring it up and wrap it around the cordage itself,

Timber hitch around first stick.

bringing it back down between the short ends of the two sticks and pull it tight. Wrap around the cordage between the sticks another two times, as tightly as you can without stressing your cordage too much; you don't want it to break! Finish it off with another couple of half-hitches. This is called **wrap and frap**

| Wrap two sticks together. | Between sticks below wrap. | Between sticks, above wrap. | Pull tight. |

and is an extremely useful method of binding two pieces of wood (or almost anything else) together. Now bind the two sticks together at the other end in this same wrap-and-frap manner.

After your sticks are tied together there should be a small gap between them of not more than one-eighth of an inch. The

binding between the two sticks will keep them from touching tight together, and that's exactly what you want. Your spindle will sit evenly over top of where the two sticks are bound side-by-side. Decide where

along the board you want your spindle to sit and use a knife or sharp rock to create a divot in the crevasse between the two

sticks. Set your coal-catcher down directly below that hole; the dust will collect there underneath. Wrap your spindle in your bow, set it in the divot and begin to bow very slowly (as described in detail in Chapter 12) to begin burning in your hole. If you move too quickly before you have burned in, your spindle will pop out. Be sure to keep your spindle perfectly vertical for the same reason!

Carve divot to seat spindle.

Once you have burned-in a full circle your spindle will be more stable and you can pick up your speed slightly. However just as when using a traditional fireboard, remember that speed is unnecessary for most of the coal-making process. (See detailed instructions on *How to Make a Coal* in Chapter 13.) Because there is no traditional notch in this two-stick

board, the dust will fall down in the gap between the two sticks. The way in which the sticks are bound side-by-side create an "almost" triangle on the bottom that is sort of like a vertical

version of the traditional notch. This is why a coal can be created using this arrangement.

As the triangular space beneath the board begins to fill with dust, it will start to build up on top of the board as well as falling through the gap. When you see a good dust build-up around your spindle get ready to start your Ten Quick Strokes (Chapter 12) to light up your coal. Then, use the spindle pumping action to help push hot air through to the coal-catcher, just as you would when making a coal on a traditional board.

This is not by any means a simple way to make fire, and it requires quite a bit of practice and persistence to become proficient and consistent using a two-stick board. However when done correctly it is not unusual to

Board turned over to show dust built up underneath.

end up with two, or even three coals; one underneath your board, and one on either side of your spindle in a ring coal. Because of this it is certainly worth the practice it takes to get the hang of, and is yet another great tool to have in your fire-making toolbox.

Handhold

As we discussed in Chapter 4, your handhold can be made of pretty much anything that fits comfortably in your hand. There are many options out there that will work exactly as you pick them up, including caps from large acorns, chunks of thick bark, pieces of wood, naturally-indented animal bones, soapstone, beach stones that have water-caused holes in them, and plenty of things I've never even thought of, I'm sure. You can also re-purpose bits of trash we humans have left behind, such as the bottom corners of broken glass bottles (be VERY careful not to cut yourself!) the tops of plastic soda or water bottles that still have a screw cap, tin can bottoms (again, be very careful not to cut yourself on the sharp edges) and who knows what else.

Handholds can be made from anything that is of a large enough diameter that it won't abrade against the sides of your spindle, and that either won't cause any friction with your spindle top (like soapstone, rock or glass) or can be lubricated well enough not to burn through. So long as it is comfortable in your hand and ***not too large***, it can be a handhold.

ॐॐॐ

"Found materials are no excuse for sloppy work."

ॐॐॐॐॐ

~ 11 ~

Using Natural Cordage

We already talked about using natural, found materials for your bow and cordage in Chapter 3, so won't re-cover that ground here. What we *are* going to go over is the different manner in which many natural material cordages must be strung on your bow and used in order to produce consistent results.

As we talked about in the chapter on *Building Your Bow*, most natural cordages can not handle the tension and/or abrasion required to be strung in the traditional manner of nylon cord. Trying to string your natural cordage bow in the same high-tension, high abrasion way you string your nylon cordage bow is failure waiting to happen. With most natural cordage materials you will be better off using either the *Tilted Bow* or *Multiple Wrap* techniques if you want to achieve consistent success.

Both of these techniques are somewhat difficult and awkward to begin with, and most people will require a fair bit of practice to do them with ease. I strongly recommend practicing these methods using cotton or jute string to begin with so you can get the movements and techniques down before moving to your own-made cordage that took time, effort and energy to make. With both of these methods, **cordage management** is the key to success, and that's not always as easy as it sounds. But if you are patient and persistent, and stay focused on slow and smooth instead of worrying about speed, you will get there.

The Tilted Bow method breaks all the rules of good bowing form, but as the saying goes, sometimes rules are made to be broken. The traditional parallel-to-the-ground bow with a single wrap of cordage around your spindle causes the cordage to rub back and forth on itself with every turn. Many natural fibers can not take this constant abrasion and will quickly fray and break. If you are going to keep using just a single wrap of string around your spindle then it is best to keep the wrapped sections of cord from touching each other, so they will not abrade, fray and break. You can do this by tilting your bow so that the tip of the bow is

Keep bow tilted at this same angle, pushing forward, not down, with each stroke. Keep your hand and bow tips moving parallel to the ground.

Do not allow your hand to move closer to the ground along the angle line of the bow. If your bow hits the ground in front of you, you are moving your bow down instead of forward at the correct, constant, angle.

closer to the ground, while the end of the bow you are holding stays higher up in the air, keeping this angle constant and parallel to the ground as you bow.

In the upcoming section on *Proper Form* we have photos showing what happens when your bow is tilted in the fashion — your string travels continuously up and down the spindle, from the top near the handhold to the bottom by the notch. In this case that is what we *want* to have happen, because this stops the cord sections from touching, and abrading against each other.

The difficulties with this method are two-fold. First, when you wrap your spindle into your cord it can not be wrapped as tight as it is with nylon string. With nylon string your spindle is wrapped so tight that it will not move along the string. For the *Tilted Bow* technique, that will not work. If you tried to keep your string that tight the spindle would constantly pop out of your board, because the tilt of the bow would create an imbalance of tension. Instead you must loosen your cord just enough that the spindle *will* move along the string. Find the tension where your spindle can easily stand upright in the socket hole while you are holding your bow at the correct tilt.

Natural cordage wrapped loosely enough that spindle can easily stay upright.

However, because your string is now so loose that you can move your bow without turning your spindle, you must add extra tension by holding the bow out, away from the spindle and your body, just far enough to allow your spindle to move, but not so far that you will pull your spindle out of your fireboard all together. You can also add extra string tension by moving your thumb or your fingers to *underneath* the string, rather than having them sitting over top. This is a delicate balancing act, and will require practice and experimentation to get just right.

Second, your bow must be tilted at the correct angle that will allow your string to travel freely up and down the spindle without touching, but not so far up or down that your string will get bound up in the handhold or fireboard, or that the tip of your bow will be scraping the ground in front of you with every stroke. This is usually about a 25-30 degree angle, and must remain consistent throughout the entire coal-making process.

I have heard some people say that this technique must be done on a downward-facing slope, or that you must be set up on top of a log or stump in order to get the angle right. Not so. It certainly can be done that way, but it is not mandatory. Doing bowdrill while facing downhill is never a great idea as you will almost always start tilting your spindle forward, which will quickly cause it to start popping out. The necessary angle is not as steep as you may think, and this is one circumstance in which using a slightly shorter bow and stroke will actually serve you better.

Bow slowly to begin, always keeping your angle at about 25-30 degrees, and watch the string go up and down the spindle. Keep the two sections of the wrap just far enough apart that they are not touching, and push your bow forward. As the cord travels, do not allow it to get any closer than about an inch from your fireboard or spindle. Slowly pull back, raising your elbow to keep the same 25-30 degree angle, while the string travels up your spindle with the cord remaining slightly separated.

Bow pulled back to tip, still tilted at 25-30° angle, allowing string to travel up close to handhold. Remember to push FORWARD, not down.

When you reach the tip of your bow (or the cord comes to within an inch of your handhold) reverse direction again.

Practice in a slow and steady manner until you can move your bow back and forth smoothly, keeping your string separated and traveling fluidly up and down the spindle. Once you feel comfortable with managing your bow and cordage, then add the necessary downward pressure and see if you can get a coal!

The Multiple Wrap is the other commonly-used technique for natural cordage in bowdrill. In this method your bow is *not* tilted, it is kept parallel to the ground. However instead of just a single time around, the *Multiple Wrap* requires at least three to five wraps of cordage around your spindle in order to be effective. (You will need a much longer cord — about twice the length of your bow — to attempt this method.)

Natural cordage wrapped five times around spindle in the Multiple Wrap style.

While many people ultimately find this multiple wrap to be easier and more versatile than the *Tilted Bow*, it does require a lot of practice and some serious cordage management! However once you get it down, the *Multiple Wrap* is an extremely effective method of working with natural cordage that can be easily modified for other methods of corded friction fire, such as mouth drill and camp drill. (Since this book is dedicated to bowdrill, we won't be covering those here).

To get set up, undo your cordage from the holding end of your bow and wrap it five times around your spindle, keeping your spindle on the outside of the string, not between the bow and the cord. Now lay your wrapped spindle down against your bow, make the string taut but not tight, and re-secure the cord to your holding end.

Just as with the *Tilted Bow* method, your cord will be loose enough that it can slide around your spindle without forcing it to turn, so you must add the extra tension yourself. Hold the bow out, away from the spindle and your body, just far enough to create the tension that will allow your spindle to move but not so far that you will pull your spindle out of your fireboard all together. Or, move your thumb or fingers *underneath* the string to create additional tension, rather than leaving them over top, or a combination of both.

In the *Tilted Bow* we kept the string-wrap at a constant distance from itself at all times to avoid string-killing abrasion. The *Multiple Wrap* works on the same principle, but in a slightly different way. The multiple wraps will move only about an inch or two up and down your spindle as you bow slowly and smoothly back and forth. They will separate just slightly, then come back together again, each time they do so.

Cordage separated as it moves along the spindle.

Once again, there are difficulties that must be overcome when using this method. First, the amount of string tension that is provided by you **must** remain constant at all times. If you allow the tension to decrease and the string to go slack, the top or bottom wrap (depending on if you are bowing forward or backward at the time) will almost immediately begin to roll over on top of the wrap below it. If you don't notice and keep bowing, your string will either get all tangled up as the wraps change their order and quickly come to a bound-up halt, or the extra abrasion caused by the overlapping movement may break your string all together.

Cordage returned together as it moves along the spindle.

Second, keeping your bow parallel to the ground is even more important in this method than it is using the traditional nylon string wrap. If you allow your bow to tilt at all, your string will overlap on itself, create a pile instead of a row, bind up and ultimately break. It is only through the steady, smooth, parallel motion of your bow that the multiple wraps will be allowd to move freely away from each other and back down into place, over and over again.

If you are having a lot of difficulty with keeping your string tight, or with overlapping, or with cordage management in general, you may want to try the *Egyptian Wrap*, which is a variation on the *Multiple Wrap* method.

Cordage that has overlapped and tangled. This must be fixed before you continue.

For the *Egyptian Wrap* style, instead of simply wrapping your string around your spindle, you begin by tying a clove hitch in the center of your bowstring and placing it around the middle of your spindle. Then, wrap your string four or five times around your spindle, above the knot (or below, but not both.) The knot will keep your cordage from slipping and from traveling as far up and down the spindle. Wrapping on only one side of the knot will greatly reduce the problem of your string binding up due to overlap.

However, depending on the length of your string and the number of wraps, you may not be able to take as long of a stroke with your bow. When using the *Egyptian-style Wrap*, be careful not to speed up your bowing; keep it slow and smooth, even if you are forced to take shorter strokes.

All of these common natural cordage methods (there are others, but these are the most common) have their advantages and disadvantages, depending on the kind of natural cordage you are using. Some types of cord will work better using a *Tilted Bow*, others with a *Multiple* or *Egyptian Wrap*. Aside from buckskin and rawhide, few very strong natural cords are able to handle the tension and abrasion of a traditional spindle wrap, at least for a long while. In order to be effective and consistent with an all-natural kit you must become effective and consistent with all of these methods. It's all about having as many tools in your tool kit as possible, and the more methods of cordage management you have perfected, the more confident and consistent all your bowdrill fire-making will become.

Out in the woods in a survival situation, it's entirely possible that you may not have the time to seek out your perfect-length spindle or to make your ideal kit. However, we have a saying that we follow here at Practical Primitive: "Practice doesn't make perfect. Perfect Practice makes perfect." By practicing finding, making and using a perfect spindle and an ideal kit, you will know exactly how everything *should* feel when you are working to make a coal. If you do ever find yourself in a true survival situation, when every moment counts and your life is on the line, the closer you can get your improvised, off-the-landscape fire kit to feeling like that perfect "at home" or lumber-yard kit, the higher your chances of being able to get that all-important, life-sustaining fire.

Thanks to your practice and experience with that ideal at-home kit you will quickly be able to recognize what doesn't feel "right" in your "survival" kit, and be able to make the necessary adjustments. If you've never known what it feels like to make fire with a great kit, you'll never know what it is that doesn't feel right in an improvised one. Using a crappy kit will produce crappy results. Fixing a crappy kit and turning it into a workable kit, will produce fire. And as we all know, in a true survival situation, Fire is Life.

"Practice doesn't make perfect. Perfect Practice makes perfect."

UNDERSTANDING

PROPER FORM

~ 12 ~

The Importance of Body Position

When it comes to easy, almost effortless, consistent coal making, proper form is key. Setting yourself up to be comfortable, stable and secure is setting yourself up for success from the very start. Even the most perfect kit can be quickly sabotaged by using lousy form. When your spindle wobbles or gets tilted; when your board is moving underfoot; when your string is going all over the place and your bow is flailing wildly; not even the best-made kit can overcome all of that. And while good form can help you to overcome a less than perfect kit, a sloppy kit combined with bad form is a recipe for bowdrill failure.

Proper bowdrill form is actually pretty simple. It is built around making sure you are comfortable and stable throughout the entire process. When you are comfortable, you can focus on your bowing rather than your balance or your sore back. When you are stable, your spindle will stay straight and drill true. Comfort and stability breed success in bowdrill and correct body position is the key to keeping proper form.

> Watch me go step-by-step through getting correctly set up in our ***Proper Bowdrill Form*** video on our Practical Primitive YouTube™ channel at https://www.youtube.com /watch?v=PlxujVPiN6U

As we go through these step-by-step instructions on form and body position I am going to assume that you already have a hole burned in and a notch cut. (See instructions for *Starting a New Hole* on pg 36 and *Carving Your Notch* on pg 37.) With the method of attaching your spindle we are using, I am also assuming that you are using nylon cord, not natural fibers.

Proper Bowdrill Form

1. Kneel down onto your dominant knee (if you are right-handed, put your right knee down, if you are left-handed, put your left knee down) and settle yourself in the "take a knee" position with one knee down on the ground and the other at 90 degrees, with your non-dominant foot flat on the ground. Make sure you are kneeling so that you form a perfect **square** between your kneeling leg, supporting leg and the ground. You should not be sitting back on your foot, or leaning way forward. You should be in a stable and comfortable position that you can easily remain in for five minutes or more. (If

Stefani is left-handed, therefore she is kneeling with her left knee down. If you are right-handed, your right knee should be on the ground.

you're like me and your knees hurt when you kneel on the ground, put a pillow under there. Remember, you need to be comfortable!) Your knee does NOT need to be directly behind your heel. That is a very unstable and awkward position and not at all conducive to good bowdrill form. Have your knee positioned  in a spot that allows you to feel stable and balanced, like you could stay there for as long as was necessary. This is usually about six to nine inches off to the side, sometimes more. When you stand in a normal comfortable position, whatever the distance is between your feet, that is about how far out to the side you will want your back knee to be in order to have that same feeling of balance.

2. Set your fireboard just in front of your foot and place your coal-catcher under the notch. (Remember, this can be a leaf, piece of bark, small bit of wood, some cardboard — anything that will allow you to easily pick up your new coal.) By the way, it makes no difference if the notch is facing you, or facing away from you. Set it up whichever way will provide the most space for your foot on the board.

3. Place your foot 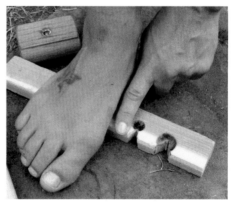 directly on top of your fireboard so that the ball of your foot is just over the far side of your board and the arch of your foot is centered on the top. Your foot should be about one finger's-width away from the hole where your spindle will be — almost as close as it can get to the spindle without actually touching it. (Tuck in pant legs and shoelaces so they don't get caught!)

4. Hold your bow in your dominant hand (if you're right-handed hold the bow in your right hand, left-handed hold it in your left hand), **all the way at the end**. By holding your bow down at the end and wrapping your hand over top of any excess string, your bowdrill cord is less likely to slip and your bow and spindle will stay more secure.

5. Grasp your spindle in your other, non-dominant hand, holding it all the way at the bottom, rounded end with the sharper, pencil-like end pointing up.

6. Near to the hand in which you are holding your bow, dive the pointed end of the spindle down in-between the string and the bow, wrap the spindle toward you, bringing it to the outside of the string, and "snap" it into an upright position with the pointier end up and the flatter end down. (Make sure your spindle is on the **outside** of the string, **NOT** between the string and the bow!) Doing this right down near your handle

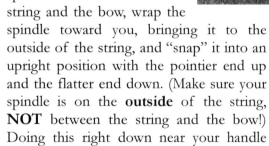

Be sure to wrap your spindle so it ends up on the **outside** of the string, not between the string and the bow. An inside wrap will compromise your ability to take long, smooth strokes.

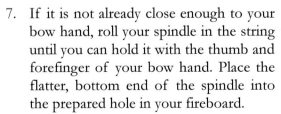

allows you to easily hold the upright spindle during the next steps.

7. If it is not already close enough to your bow hand, roll your spindle in the string until you can hold it with the thumb and forefinger of your bow hand. Place the flatter, bottom end of the spindle into the prepared hole in your fireboard.

Be sure the flatter, rounded end has been placed into the board and the pencil point end is facing up.

8. Pick up your already greased handhold in your free (non-dominant) hand and place it on top of the spindle's pointy end.

9. Watch the placement of your hand on top of your handhold. You want the force of your weight to be directly over top of the spindle, not beside it. Be sure to keep your handhold perpendicular to the spindle at all times. If your handhold is at an off-angle, your pressure is not being directed down the spindle and you will end up tilting your spindle and working much harder than necessary. To check if your hand and handhold positions are correct and properly placed, press your handhold down on your spindle then open your fingers so your palm is flat. If your spindle stays in the same position, your handhold is correctly balanced and properly positioned. If your

spindle flies out or falls over or wants to lean, your hand was not centered over the spindle and you need to re-adjust your holding placement.

10. With your handhold correctly placed, lock the inside of your wrist up against your shin so that your spindle is perfectly vertical, and **keep it there!** Adjust your placement, moving your foot and/or fireboard either forward or back as needed to get your wrist touching your shin while still keeping your spindle in a straight up-and-down position. Adjust your supporting knee as necessary to maintain your perfect square. Remember that the inside of your wrist **should ALWAYS be touching your shin!**

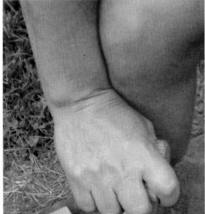

By keeping the inside of your wrist continuously locked against your shin through the entire process, you will ensure your spindle remains stable and does not wobble in the hole. This stability is important for your success! Allowing your wrist to come away from your shin forces those tiny muscles in your wrist to maintain 360 degree stability, which they absolutely cannot do.

11. Keeping your arm straight, lean your whole upper body over to press down on your handhold. This will exert all the downward pressure on your spindle that you should need. By keeping your back and arm straight and leaning with the full weight of your body, you won't have to work nearly as hard at pressing down. If you allow your arm to bend and your back to hunch over, you will be forcing yourself to use the small muscles in your wrist and forearm to create the downward pressure you need. This is a much harder way of doing things and you will tire far more quickly.

Keep your spindle arm and your back straight, and simply lean over to generate your downward pressure. Don't allow yourself to become all hunched or you'll force your wrist and forearm to do all the work.

12. With your spindle perfectly vertical, and keeping your bow parallel to the ground and at 90 degrees to the spindle, begin **slowly** moving your bow back and forth. *You do not need to come straight backward with your bow!* Allow your bow arm to angle out to the side so that it passes your

kneeling leg naturally. Be sure to use the full length of the bow with each stroke, from the far tip right back to your hand every time. "Short stroking" — only using the center of your bow instead of the full length — will cause you to want to bow faster than necessary, and to waste energy. Each time you pull your bow backward, allow your wrist to bend and your elbow to straighten. As you push forward, bend your elbow as you straighten your wrist. Moving your arm from the shoulder like a pendulum will help keep your elbow from locking up, which is what causes your bow to "saw" instead of move smoothly. If you don't bend your elbow and your wrist, your bow will not

Move your bow the entire length — from the base near your hand all the way out to the tip — with each stroke. Allow both your wrist and your elbow to bend and straighten as your bow moves forward and back.

remain parallel to the ground. Your bow tip will rise and drop, your string will travel up and down the spindle, and you will have difficulty with the entire process.

Keep your bow parallel to the ground at all times.

117

Pushing in a "sawing" motion with your elbow locked will cause the tip of your bow to rise and fall.

When your bow tip rises above your hand it causes the string to bind on itself, making it almost impossible to push your bow forward.

When the tip of the bow falls below the level of your hand, the string travels up and down the spindle.

Continued bowing in this manner will cause the string to move farther and farther up or down the spindle, causing it to eventually bind up at either the handhold or the fireboard hole.

ALWAYS KEEP YOUR BOW PARALLEL TO THE GROUND!

13. Always, always, *always* keep your spindle absolutely vertical as you continue to bow. If you allow your spindle to tilt, you will almost immediately begin to have issues. A spindle tilted forward or backward will widen the front of the hole where it meets the notch, to the point where there is not enough mass and your spindle will begin to pop out with almost every stroke. It will also cause your string to bind up on itself, making it difficult to impossible to move your bow back and forth smoothly. A sideways tilt  will cause unwanted friction to occur along the sides of the hole as you drill deeper into the fireboard, causing side friction and squeaking.

Leaning, or allowing your spindle to tilt, causes it to push forward. Very quickly the spindle will travel out to, and then past, the edge of your fire board and begin constantly popping out.

These are the basics of proper bowdrill form. Keep your knee at square, your arm straight, your handhold centered and perpendicular, your spindle vertical and your bow always parallel to the ground taking smooth, full-length strokes. Following these basic steps will completely eliminate many of the coal-killing difficulties of other set-ups. Pop-outs and side friction disappear, no more wallowing out your hole, string binding and lock-up are eliminated, and downward pressure is easy to generate because your entire upper body is in on the act. By setting yourself up with this balanced and proper form you will be setting yourself up for success every time.

One last note on proper form before we move on to actually creating a coal. The older I get, the more it hurts my knees to get down on the ground to do bowdrill. Let me ask you this; where is it written that I have to? Not in this book, that's for sure! As long as you are stable and square, there is no reason whatsoever that you must do bowdrill on the ground. Find a bench, chair, stump, rock or whatever you can find that is the appropriate height and set your kit up on top of that. Instead of making a square with your bent knee on the ground, you are now making a rectangle. Your knee is still bent at that 90 degree angle, you are just keeping your other leg straight instead of getting down on one knee.

If you have trouble with pain or stability when practicing bowdrill kneeling, I highly recommend getting

Putting your foot up on a log, stump or bench of the correct height keeps your Proper Form square, but is easier on your back and knees. Many people feel more stable in this position. (But keep your arm straight!)

yourself up off the ground and giving it a try this way. Many of our students have gone from frustrated failure to quick success, simply by moving their kit onto our picnic bench rather than remaining painfully and awkwardly on the ground.

Remember that comfort and stability are the watch words for proper form. Oh, and don't forget to breathe!

"Comfort and stability breed success in bowdrill and correct body position is the key to keeping proper form."

~ *13* ~

How to Make a Coal

All right boys and girls, this is it, what we've all been waiting for. We've been through the how's and the why's of making friction fire work; we've built a proper-sized kit, carved a perfect notch, made up an easy-to-light tinder bundle and practiced our proper form. Now it's time to put it all together and make ourselves a coal. So let's get to it!

No matter what method you are using, be it bowdrill, hand drill, fire saw or whatever, all friction fire is created using the same three step process:

1. Warm Up Your Kit
2. Generate Your Dust
3. Ignite Your Dust into a Coal

Let's take a look at each step in detail, so you understand how each phase works and why it is so important.

Step 1 — Warm up your kit

You can't have fire without heat (remember the Fire Triangle!) and with bowdrill you generate that heat through friction. It takes time to build up that heat — not much, but at least a few seconds, depending on the ambient weather conditions — and you must take that time in order to be successful. During this step, speed is irrelevant, and can even be detrimental under certain circumstances. When you first begin to bow, a slow, steady rhythm, back and forth, back and forth, will serve you best. For students who have difficulty getting or keeping a good rhythm I'll usually start to sing the children's song, *"I'm a Little Tea Pot"*. It sounds silly, but it works!

I'm a little tea pot, short and stout,
Here is my handle, here is my spout.
When I get all steamed up here me shout,
Tip me over and pour me out.

Each beat of the song is one stroke. It keeps you on pace and your rhythm steady and stops you from going too fast, or from sawing through the process all unevenly. All you are doing right now is warming up your kit, and there is absolutely no need to

bow as fast as you can, or to wear yourself out. You are just in Stage 1, so slow down and don't work so hard!

Once you begin to see a thin tendril of smoke snaking its way up from where your spindle and fireboard meet, you know your kit is warm, and you are now beginning to generate dust.

Why is it not a good idea to bow fast and work hard right from the start? First of all, it is a completely unnecessary expenditure of energy, which, in a survival situation, you cannot afford. But even when you are

The tendril of smoke where the spindle and fireboard meet tells you that your kit is warm and you are now entering Step 2: Generating dust.

123

practicing at home, working too fast too quickly can actually be detrimental under certain conditions. On days when there is a lot of ambient moisture in the air, such as the high heat and humidity of summer, or before or after a rain, working too hard too soon can ruin your chances of making a coal.

When it comes to fire, Rule #1 is "Wet stuff doesn't burn." Many woods that work very well for bowdrill also like to soak up that humidity (cedar is a good example) and if you start immediately bowing with all your speed, energy and might, you will start creating dust too soon. Too soon because your materials are still damp. This means that you are creating dust from damp wood, therefore your dust is also damp. If your kit has absorbed humidity, and you don't take the time to push out that moisture through a slow build up of heat, then all that dust you are creating is just as damp as your fire kit. Damp dust does not like to create a coal. Remember Rule #1 — Wet stuff doesn't burn — and that includes the dust you make in bowdrill.

By starting with that slow, steady, back and forth bowing you will build heat gradually, driving out any humidity and moisture that may have built up in your kit. With the moisture gone the dust you generate will be both warm AND dry, and your coal will be far more likely to ignite.

Step 2 — Generate dust

Now that your kit is warm you are starting to generate dust. Hooray! Once again, at this stage, speed is irrelevant. Over and over and over I'll see bowdrill videos where people are bowing as fast as they can and wearing themselves out, and none of it is necessary!

You will need to fill your entire notch up with dust before you're going to get a coal, so take your time. Slow and steady. Conserve your energy for when you really need it. Saying that you need to bow as fast as you can while you generate your dust is like saying that in order for your fire to light, you need to run around the woods as fast as you can to collect your firewood. Because that is all you are doing during this stage, gathering firewood.

Remember back to your Fire Triangle. Your dust is your fuel, and before anything is going to happen you will need to have a nice big pile of that dark brown dust, all falling on top of itself in the confined space that is your notch, with just enough oxygen available through the front of the board. Once enough of that hot dust has gathered together into a pile, it will reach its ignition temperature and, essentially, self-ignite. Then you'll have your coal! But you need to have enough dust for this to happen.

"How much dust is enough?" "How long do I need to keep bowing?" "How do I tell when I'm done?" These are the questions I hear most often at this stage and I will tell you what I

tell them. ***Keep bowing until the entire notch is full to overflowing with dust.*** Until you see the dust building up around your spindle, and then falling out of the front of the notch. A larger pile of dust will ignite into a coal at a lower temperature than a smaller pile will, so you want to have a nice big pile sitting there, looking like a little worm crawling out of your board.

Keep bowing until the dust is falling out of your notch on to your coal catcher. The more dust you have, the larger your coal, the easier to blow into flame.

Keep that slow, steady, *"I'm a little tea pot"* rhythm the entire time and, provided you are using the correct size of spindle, you will fill your entire notch with relative ease in just a few minutes, without even breathing hard. Three times through the song is usually all you need to generate your dust. Sometimes a little longer, sometimes a little less, but three times is a pretty good guide. If you can't easily hold a conversation (or sing a little song) while you are generating your dust, you are working too hard. Remember, at this point in the process, *SPEED IS IRRELEVANT!*

Step 3 — Ignite the dust

Now that your notch is full-to-overflowing with beautiful dark brown dust, it's time to ignite your coal. The fact is that you may already have a coal, without having used any speed at all. (We call this *"slow-drill"* and have entire contests built around creating a bowdrill coal while bowing as slow as you possibly can.) But if you do need to light your dust, now is the time. Ready? Ten Quick Strokes. GO!!

Keep doing everything *exactly* the same way you have been doing it all along — full-length, easy, smooth strokes, your bow staying parallel to the ground, your spindle staying vertical and your wrist locked in against your shin. Don't increase your pressure! Continue to use just enough pressure to keep your set from squeaking. Squeaking at this stage can send a sound shock wave down into your dust and blow your whole coal apart. All you need to do is speed up your bowing arm to about twice as fast as you were going while you generated your dust. During your Ten Quick Strokes you will be creating a lot of smoke and

that's a good thing! That extra heat from the additional speed will kick the level of heat inside your pile of dust into overdrive, taking it up to combustion temperature and turning it into a coal. Hooray!

After you have completed your Ten Quick Strokes, stop bowing, take your hand off your bow and put it down on your fireboard to hold it in place. (Your bow will be fine just hanging there around the spindle for a few moments.) Then, and *only* then, *carefully* lift your foot off the board *while keeping your hand on the board and leaving your spindle in place*. There is nothing sadder than going through all that work and effort to create a coal, then lifting your foot and spindle up all at the same time, accidentally shoving the board forward and breaking up your coal. So upsetting! I know you are very excited and want to see that coal, but take a breath and be careful. More coals are destroyed in this moment than at any other time during bowdrill.

Once you have carefully taken your foot off the board, use your bow hand to hold your spindle while you set down your handhold. Now quickly and carefully lift the spindle out of the hole and unwrap it from the bow, then set it gently back down in

the hole and carefully and gently pump your spindle up and down in the hole a few times. These are just small, gentle little pumps that barely even touch your board. Your goal here is to push an extra blast of hot air down through the dust, and to further increases the heat at the center of your coal. (Think of a bellows on a fire.) This can also help to push an "on the edge" coal over into life, or keep a coal going during poor weather conditions. As you are doing those few gentle spindle pumps to push through that extra hot air, carefully tilt your fireboard up and away from your coal. (Pumping the spindle will also help to release the coal from the notch if it is a little bit stuck to the wood.) Set your fireboard

back down right next to your coal.

Carefully lift up your coal-catcher with the coal sitting on top of it and set the whole thing right up on top of your fireboard, directly over the hole you were just using. The heat coming up from the hole, through the coal-catcher and into your coal from the bottom, will help to keep it hot and growing.

Don't forget this step. It may seem unimportant but on more than one occasion I have watched coals dissipate and die because all the heat was pulled out of the coal and into the cold ground. Remember, cold steals heat. At this stage your coal is still quite fragile and leaving it on the cold ground, or cold wood, or cold stone, or cold floor is begging for disaster. The heat can be sucked right out of your coal, leaving you with a lovely pile of dust, but nothing more.

Beautiful finished coal consolidating on top of the fireboard.

Presuming that you do have a coal, (hooray for you!) and you have successfully taken your foot off the fireboard, lifted the board away from the coal and picked the coal up off the ground so it is sitting on top of the hole in the board, now is the time to **let it sit**. There is no need to rush at this point. Your coal will happily burn away for five minutes or more if you just leave it where it is on top of the board, so you have plenty of time. (A coal left on the cold ground will disappear quickly, not because it burns up faster, but because the heat is sucked out into the cold ground.)

Remember, your newly formed coal is a very small and very

How do you know if you have a coal?

Once you have stopped bowing and carefully removed your fireboard, if your dust continues to smoke, you have a coal.

If the smoke stops, after the fireboard is taken away, you do not have a coal. Don't despair! Just put your fireboard back in place, re-warm your dust (basically an extended version of Step 1) and go through the ignition process once again. Or, even better, set your old dust aside and begin again with Step 1.

fragile little thing at the center of your pile of dust. By rushing to transfer your coal into your tinder bundle too soon, you can easily break your coal apart into tiny pieces that won't blow easily, or at all, into flame. So be patient once again, and allow your coal to sit, coalesce and grow before you try to move it.

As your coal sits and grows you will notice that the little tendril of smoke will begin to get stronger and thicker, and maybe a little more yellow-looking in color. Soon after that you will see, some place on the coal, a spot of red, like the "cherry" on the end of a lit cigarette. NOW your coal is strong and solid and ready to be moved.

Carefully pick up your prepared tinder bundle in one hand, and your coal-catcher in the other. CAREFULLY turn your coal-catcher sideways and drop your coal, along with any extra dust, into the center of your tinder bundle. DO NOT shake your coal-catcher! The shaking can still break up your fragile coal, or you may accidentally hit your coal with your coal-catcher and break it apart. Just turn your coal-catcher sideways and allow everything to drop into your tinder bundle. If

Notice how thick the smoke is and see the small spot of red at about the 8 o'clock position in the dust pile.

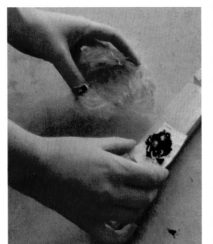

you discover that your coal is stuck to your coal-catcher, give a gentle tap on the side to dislodge it, or turn the entire thing completely upside-down and tap the bottom with your finger until the coal drops off.

Position yourself so that your back is to the wind. You are about to begin "blowing up" your tinder bundle and you don't want all that smoke blowing straight into your face and choking you as you try to take your next breath. Notice which way the smoke is moving, and face your body so that the smoke is blowing *away* from you.

Anatomy of a Coal

For pyrolysis (coal ignition) to occur, your dust must reach an internal temperature of 450-500°F. We pointed an instant thermometer at the notch for the entirety of the coal-creation process to view the *external* temperatures required. Here is what we saw.

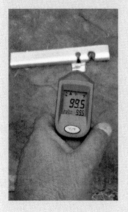

1. Prior to beginning, the area within the notch was 99.5° F. It was a hot summer day and the ambient temperature of the stone on which the fireboard is sitting is reflected in this temperature.

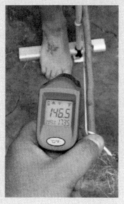

2. Once Stefani began to generate dust, the notch temperature quickly shot up to over 140° F.

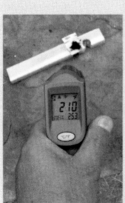

3. The coal was born at 160° F.

4. As the coal sat to consolidate, the temperature rose to over 210° F.

5. The red spot telling us the coal was stable and ready to transfer to the tinder bundle appeared at about 250° F.

Blowing Your Tinder Into Flame

Now that your coal and extra dust are in your tinder bundle, you are starting your fire triangle all over again. This time, your coal provides the heat, your tinder is the fuel and you will be providing the oxygen with your blowing. (Technically, since our exhaled breaths are carbon dioxide, the blowing causes constant airflow containing oxygen to move through the tinder bundle, but you get the idea.) Since, as the laws of physics dictate, no fire is going to happen until the fuel (in this case, your tinder) reaches its ignition temperature, it is okay to let your coal just sit there in your tinder for a few seconds. This will allow your tinder to begin warming up, which is *especially* important on cold, damp, humid or rainy days, as the hair-fine tinder material will readily absorb those ambient weather conditions. Blowing on your coal before your tinder has had a chance to warm up will waste the coal's energy and you may blow out the coal before your tinder catches on fire. So once again, take your time!

Remember, your goal is to get your tinder bundle to catch on fire, so please, please, *please* do not hold it cupped in your two hands! Hold your tinder bundle with just your fingertips, and bring it up to the height of your face. Gently fold your bird's nest bundle over into more of a taco shape, pressing carefully so that the tinder is touching the coal. Don't squeeze too tight — you don't want to crush your coal. Hold it so that the tinder is in direct contact with the coal, but softly, like you are holding a baby bird in a blanket.

Position your tinder bundle so that it is level with your nose, and about a hand span away from your face. If your tinder bundle is too close to your mouth, the moisture and carbon dioxide from your breath may have an adverse effect, so keep it six to nine inches, or about a hand span, away. Carefully open your tinder taco to the point where you can see your coal, and blow. Not timid little soft blows — those will not provide the force of air needed to bring your fire to life. You need to blow good, strong, "birthday candle" blows. Imagine that you are trying to blow out twenty candles on a birthday cake — you would need to blow a long, steady stream of air to try and get them all. This is the same type of blowing your coal needs to get hot enough to cause

The more red you see, the harder you can blow!

your tinder to burst into flame. Blow right on to your coal. Make it turn red. The more red you see, the harder you can blow.

As your coal gets redder and redder it will continually eat up the fuel immediately surrounding it, so be sure to keep enough gentle pressure on your tinder bundle to keep the tinder always in contact with your coal. You will see more and more smoke start to come out of your tinder, and it will get thicker and thicker with each strong blow. Remember, smoke is incomplete combustion, so the

more smoke you see and the thicker that smoke is, the closer you are to having fire. When the smoke is thick and yellow-ish, get ready because you are about to have FIRE!

When your tinder bundle bursts into flame, do your best not to throw it away, or drop it down onto your fire kit! It's hard, I know, because we are not used to having something burning right there in our bare hands, and our instinct is to get rid of it as quickly as possible! This will almost certainly happen at least the first few times, but an important part of fire making is learning to overcome this instinct. The

Try not to throw your flaming tinder bundle down onto anything important!

ultimate purpose of this entire endeavor, from making your kit to creating your coal to blowing your tinder up into flame, is to actually start a fire. So when your tinder ignites, practice placing it down on the ground in a calm and deliberate manner. When you have the time and the appropriate space, build a fire structure and practice actually lighting it by placing your tinder bundle into the structure itself.

Congratulations! You did it! You made fire! After all the kit building, all the fixing up and adjusting, all the practice, and the wondering if it's going to work, if it really can be done, if you really can do it, you, my friend, have made a coal! Let me tell you, there is no feeling quite like that moment when your first tinder bundle bursts into flame right there in your hands!

If you're like me, and I hope you are, then the first thing you're going to want to do after making your first coal is rest for a few minutes, and try it again! Before you do, it is important to

This spindle has drilled deep into the board, which is now creating *side friction*. Notice how tight the top of the hole is around the spindle.

take a few moments to check over your kit and get it re-set before starting again. Feel the pointy top of your spindle. Is it still shiny and smooth? Do you need to add more soap or grease into your handhold? What about the bottom of your spindle? Has it gotten too rounded? Is it too flat? Does it have a pointy nipple in the middle? Bring it back into that nice, slightly

Carving away the top edge of the hole frees the spindle and eliminates side friction. Your spindle will now move noticeably easier.

135

Why Does My Kit Squeak?

Bowdrill kits squeak for only two reasons: N*ot enough downward pressure* or *side friction.*

A lack of downward pressure is the most common cause of squeaking. For successful bowdrill you need to use just enough downward pressure to stop the squeak, and no more. If you are getting a squeak, increase your downward pressure until the squeaking stops. If you know you are pressing down hard enough, or if you see that the increased pressure is beginning to cause hairs or platelets instead of dust, *side friction* may be your problem.

Side friction squeaking can be coming from either your handhold or your fireboard and there are a couple of possibilities at each end. First, think back to how long ago you last lubricated your handhold. If it's been a while, that may be your problem. If your handhold is well greased, tilt it slightly in a different direction. You may be holding it a little off-center and hearing your spindle rubbing against the edge of the handhold hole.

To check your fireboard, adjust the tilt of your spindle. If you are not holding it perfectly vertical it could be rubbing against the side of the socket hole. If your spindle is vertical, look at the depth of the hole. If you are getting side friction between the sides of your spindle in a deep socket hole, carve open the top of the hole as described on the previous page in order to stop the squeaking.

Whatever the reason your kit is squeaking, you MUST figure it out and you MUST stop it from happening. Every squeak sends a sound shock wave down into your pile of dust that causes the individual particles to jump and push apart. This jumping stops your dust from compacting together and inhibits the formation of your coal. As long as there is squeaking, there will be no coal forming, so find it, fix it, then start again.

curved shape like the back of a spoon. How about your fireboard? Do you need to start a new hole? Do you have enough wood to make another coal or have you drilled almost through to the very bottom of your board? (Most holes in a medium-hard fireboard are good for three to five fires, give or take.) How deep is your current hole? Is it deep enough that you are going to get side friction this time? Take a look at your spindle and see if there is dark brown or black coming up the sides (meaning that the sides of the spindle were rubbing tightly against the sides of the hole and creating unhelpful friction along the edges.) Do you need to carve away the top edge of the hole to allow the spindle to move freely? Do you have your next tinder bundle ready?

These are the questions to ask yourself every time you pick up your kit in preparation for creating a coal. Remember back in Chapter 1 when I talked about noticing that every time Eddie picked up his kit, he worked with it, adjusted it and prepared it before he began? These are the things he was checking. These are the things that I check every time I prepare to make fire. These are the things that you will check too, because now you, too, know that fire isn't magic. It is magical.

&&&

Congratulations!
You did it! You made fire!

&&&&&

~ 14 ~

Does This Really Work? Really?

I'm sure that by now you're asking yourself, "Does this really work?" I mean sure, it sounds all good on paper, but if this is such a great and easy way for anyone to make bowdrill successfully and reliably, then why doesn't everyone teach it this way? Why doesn't every internet video show it done this way? Why do so many survival experts on television shows always make it look so difficult?

Valid questions, to be sure, and ones that I can't answer except to say that there are a lot of people out there doing bowdrill, experts or not, who don't yet have a full understanding of *why* it works. But I promise you that it does, indeed, work. Here at Practical Primitive we have been teaching bowdrill in exactly this fashion for over eight years now, with a 100% success rate. That's right, 100% success. *Every single person* who has come through our fire-making workshops, our demonstrations, our instruction on how to make a bowdrill coal, has actually made a bowdrill coal. From high school kids to retirees, from big strong men to little old ladies, even people with physical limitations, disabilities and amputees. Every single person who has followed our instruction and didn't give up has gotten a coal. Usually in 30 minutes or less.

Many times we have had students who did not believe that what we told them actually worked, including people who had already been doing bowdrill for however long, with moderate or even fairly regular success. People who figured that what they were doing was already mostly working so what could we have to say that would make it any better? We give them a kit and tell them to go for it and watch their form and technique to see what they can do. Even when they are able to make a coal, about 99.9% of the time they are working way too hard. I cannot even count the number of times I have had to tell people to slow down, to ease up, to stop working so hard! Remember, when the physics are correct, when your kit is the right size for your body, bowdrill is virtually effortless and virtually always successful.

Many of the folks who are working so hard are strong, fit young men who can simply "power through". Basically, they can just go and go and go and go until they get a coal. They use all the strength and stamina and energy they have to "force" a coal into existence. Which is fine I suppose. The point is to get a coal, so if you can get a coal, no matter how you do it, that is success!

But what happens when you can't? What happens if you're tired? If you're sick? If you're injured or calorie-deprived or dehydrated? If you've been in an accident, or when you just get older?

Now obviously we don't learn these skills in the expectation of being lost in the jungle or crashed in the mountains or broken down on the African savannah, or in whatever simulated "survival" situation comes up on the many, many television shows these days. We do these skills because they're fun! But the truth is that every year there are people who find themselves in what we call "Uh-Oh" events. People who get lost while they're hiking, who break down in the desert, who turn down a closed road and get stuck... People find themselves in what could easily turn into "Survival" situations almost every day. Sometimes those situations resolve quickly and everyone goes home with a great story to tell at their next party, and sometimes we hear about them on the news.

Let's use these Survival shows as an example. How often do we watch as someone who claims they have "no problem" getting fire-by-friction, that they have been doing it for years and are, let's face it, a "fire god". Then we watch them fail and fail and fail and they have no idea why they are having problems. Why it isn't working the same way it always has before. If you watch them you will see that they are counting on their power, their strength and their stamina. They are used to "powering through" and now that they are tired, hungry, dehydrated and a little scared, that just doesn't work.

Survival is a numbers game. If you take in more calories than you put out, you survive. If you expend more calories than you replace, you will slowly starve to death and die. In a survival situation, *Metabolic Efficiency* must be your abiding rule. Every calorie you burn matters. And when you try to "power through" to make a coal, you are unnecessarily expending a huge number of those precious calories.

By understanding the physics of fire, by correctly sizing your kit, by reading your dust and listening and responding to what fire is telling you, by using proper form and this simple 3-step method of coal-creation, you will use the fewest number of calories you can, lose the smallest amount of fluid possible (by not sweating because you are not expending so much energy) and have the highest probability of success in actually getting that desperately needed coal.

Power is great, if you have it. But the day will come when you don't. And if power is the only tool in your toolbox, then you don't really have any tools at all. If power is the only way you can get fire, then you don't know fire at all.

So the short answer is yes, this does really work. If you will build your kit to match your body; if you will take the time to make your kit as perfect as you can; if you will cut your notch the proper size and shape and put it in the proper place; and if you will fix your form and watch and read your dust and follow the steps as I've described them, you can do this. You *will* do this!

One of my favorite success stories is also one of my first. One of the students in our 6-month *World of the Hunter-Gatherer* Intensive Skills Program had been practicing primitive skills for a couple of years when she began the program, and had never once been able to get a coal using her bowdrill kit. She wasn't even getting any dust and was pretty convinced that she couldn't do it. She may even have been told that she was just too small; that she didn't have enough upper body strength to do bowdrill. (Which, as you all know by now, is complete baloney!) Though to her credit, she kept on trying!

We had Lara bring along the bowdrill kit she had been using so we could troubleshoot what was going on and get her on track to getting a coal. It took about two seconds of looking at her kit to understand why she had never been successful. Remember the rule about how your spindle should be about the size of your thumb? Well Lara is small-boned. Her thumb is about the size of my pinky. But her spindle was closer to the size of her wrist! Okay, that might be a slight exaggeration, but not by much. The spindle she had been working with all this time was at least an inch in diameter, probably more. There was NO WAY this woman was EVER going to be able to make a coal using that spindle. It was not physically possible. She was 100% incapable of generating the amount of downward pressure that was required to make the chocolate brown dust of a coal. It was NEVER going to happen!

We took her giant-sized spindle away, gave her a spindle that was less than half the diameter of the one she'd been using and had her go again. Bam. There was the dust she had never been able to make. We fixed up the notch in her fireboard, making it a little deeper into the hole and widening it out to the proper 45 degrees and had her start again. Bam. That chocolate brown dust was now falling right down into the notch exactly where it needed to be. We adjusted her form to make her more comfortable and stable and keep her spindle straight and solid and had her start again. Bam. Coal. She had been trying and trying and trying for years without success, and within 20 minutes of using the principles, rules and methods laid out in this book and she had her very first coal.

Sarah's story is very similar. She had been working on getting a bowdrill coal for over a year. She even spent a few months living primitively full-time, trying day after day to get a coal, without success. Needless to say that by the time she came to us she was beyond frustrated and almost certain that it was just not possible for her. Once again, with a quick look at her kit it was obvious that she had been working with a spindle that was much too large. We swapped out her spindle for one that was appropriately-sized to her frame, fixed up her notch and adjusted her form. Her very first try, Sarah had her very first coal.

Sarah, triumphant, after making her first bowdrill coal.

Now most people who get their first coal after having struggled for so long are thrilled with having created that beautiful red glow; not Sarah. After the initial excitement passed, Sarah was furious! She could not believe that it was so easy, and no one had told her. She was furious that, out of everyone she had learned from, everyone who had watched her try, everyone who had coached her on bowdrill over the past year, none of them had told her these few basics things that made all the difference between months of continued failure, and the quick, easy success she had finally achieved. Since that day in 2009, Sarah has made it her mission to spread the word. She is determined that no one else ever have the same frustrating, agonizing and completely unnecessary beginner bowdrill experience that she did.

I could go on and on with story after story of long-time frustration being turned quickly into success. There was Pat, for whom we had to keep dropping her spindle size until we were down to just 3/8" before she finally was able to get her coal. Jason, who thought that he had to press down as hard as he possibly could and bow as fast as possible at all times, and as a result had been producing nothing but coal-killing platelets while exhausting himself by working about five times harder than necessary. We slowed down his bowing and kept repeating "less pressure, less pressure, less pressure" over and over and over again until he had finally eased up enough to get that beautiful dark brown dust, and his first coal. Rob, who had been carving his notches so wide that his spindle had been constantly popping out front. With a proper-sized notch, he started cranking out coals like a machine.

Over and over and over again, we see the same problems, the same frustrations, the same failures. We change the spindle size, fix the notch, adjust the form, and turn those failures into successes. Every... single... time.
And you will too!

One of the things I am constantly telling people who are new to bowdrill, and to friction fire in general, is to always remember that "it's way easier than they make it look on TV." I find it so very sad and frustrating to hear people who call themselves "instructors" talking about how friction fire is extremely difficult; that it is a real specialty skill; that only the strongest could ever make fire; that fire-by-friction is only 30-40% reliable... On and on and on, over and over and over again, I hear people who are supposed to be experts in their field pass along bad information that only highlights just how much they don't know about fire, and don't understand about the rules and laws and physics of how fire works.

It is my hope that, now that you DO know the rules and laws and physics of fire, and DO understand how and *why* bowdrill works, that you, too, will create your own relationship with fire that will bring you success and consistency, as well as the confidence to know that you can create fire with a bowdrill, virtually every time.

My own journey with fire has been a long and winding one. Over the past 11 years I have gone from being amazed and astounded, to confused and frustrated, to over-confident and subsequently humbled, to strong and sure in my abilities. I have learned the truth to the saying that Fire is Magical, but it is not magic.

Troubleshooting Questions

The methods laid out in this book are proven, as the many hundreds and thousands of people who use them can attest. If you are ready to be able to create a coal using a bowdrill virtually every single time; if you are ready to understand that it really isn't that hard; if you are ready 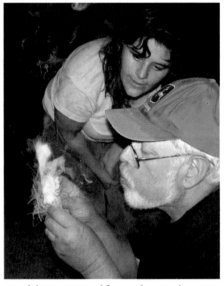 to realize that the type of wood you are using rarely makes a difference; and if you are ready to succeed and build your own sure and confident relationship with fire, then I encourage you to get out there and do this stuff!

The number one reason that people don't make fire with a bowdrill is that they are afraid to try; afraid to not succeed. Of course you will be unsuccessful! If you're not pushing yourself to the point you don't succeed, you will never learn anything new. Everyone fails to succeed. Eddie fails, I fail, and you will fail. What people tend to forget is that not succeeding is different from failure. Failure is giving up. Failure is making the same mistakes over and over without learning from them. Failure is admitting defeat before you even begin.

Lack of success is never an excuse to quit, or to not try at all. The times you don't succeed are simply guideposts along the road to your eventual success. When you try to make a bowdrill coal, and you fail to succeed (because you will), take the time to consider *why* you failed. What needs to be adjusted in order to achieve success? Ask yourself the following questions:

- How was my form? Was I stable and balanced?
- Was my spindle straight up and down, my wrist sturdy against my shin, or was everything wobbling around?
- Is my spindle straight and round or was it chattering? Was I leaning, causing my spindle to travel on the board or pop out?
- What does my dust look like? Is it that perfect dark chocolate color? Did I create dust? Or do I have hairs? Or platelets? Do I need to adjust my downward pressure or the size of my spindle?
- Was I squeaking? If so, was the squeak coming from my handhold? (Was I holding it off kilter or does it need more lubrication?) Was it coming from my fireboard? (Was it being caused by side friction or do I need to press down a little harder?)
- If I wasn't pressing down hard enough, did I "glaze over"? Do I need to break that glaze?
- Is my dust falling down into my notch or is it instead building up around my spindle? If so, is my notch the correct size and in the optimal place?
- Do I have enough dust? Did I keep bowing until the notch was completely full and dust was falling out the front like a worm, or did I stop too soon?
- Did I keep everything stable and not increase my pressure when I did my Ten Quick Strokes?
- Did I carefully remove my foot so as not to kick my board and break apart my coal?

- Did I lift my coal-catcher up off the ground and onto my board so the cold ground wouldn't steal my newborn coal's heat?
- Was I patient enough in allowing my coal to consolidate, waiting until I saw red before transferring it to my tinder bundle?
- Did I allow my tinder the chance to warm up before I began to blow on my coal?
- Did I keep my tinder gently pressed against my coal, and give good, strong, birthday-candle blows?
- Was my tinder dry, hair-fine, and easy to light?

These are the questions I ask myself every time a coal doesn't appear, or won't blow into flame. Every single time the answer to what went wrong is somewhere in there; I just have to take the time to figure out what needs to be adjusted, to fix it, and start again to achieve success.

If you will invest the time, effort and energy into discovering where the adjustments need to be made, whether it is in your kit or in your form, then you, too, will realize just how simple, effortless and reliable bowdrill fire can truly be. Every Single Time.

"We change the spindle size, fix the notch, adjust the form, and turn those failures into successes. Every... Single... Time."

~ 15 ~

The Magic of Fire

Thursday April 7
7:09 p.m.
I MADE FIRE!!
I MADE FIRE! TWICE! How can I begin to express that feeling? I can't. I won't bother to try. But I walk differently now. I see the world differently. I connected in a very tangible way with the ancients; the ancestors. I am changed.

That is the entry in my journal from back in 2005, after the very first time I ever made fire with a bowdrill kit. It was a warm spring evening at a survival school in the redwood forest near Santa Cruz. Dinner was over and the next lecture would be starting soon. There were only 15 minutes now until I was to be back in my seat to learn more about building primitive shelters and I was down on one knee, sawing away, trying yet again to get that elusive little coal to appear. Ten minutes to go now, and my frustration was starting to build. While I felt like I was getting closer and closer, there was still nothing every time I took away my board. By this point I had burned down through to the bottom of my hole and needed to cut a new notch. This time I got help from one of the instructors rather than carving my own, so my notch was actually the proper size and shape! Five minutes left until class was re-starting, and the pressure was on. Everyone was heading back into the lecture hall. It was getting dark and I

147

was pretty much ready to give up yet again. But Mike, one of the volunteers for that class, stuck with me, generously offering encouragement; telling me to keep going, to not give up, that I could do it! So I decided to give it one more try.

This time, something felt different. There was no more squeaking. I was getting more dust. Everything seemed to be falling into place. The call came to "Come on in" and I began to panic. Mike told me to forget about the lecture and just keep going. So I did.

I kept bowing and bowing; I was getting tired, sweat was dripping off my nose from the humidity. The pressure of knowing the class was starting without me was weighing me down, but with Mike's encouragement I just kept going. When I finally stopped, there was a perfectly huge pile of dark brown dust, and there it was; that little tendril of smoke snaking out from the center.

I had a coal!!!!

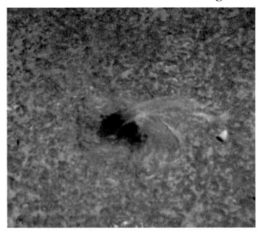

My muscles were so tired I couldn't make them work properly and my hands were shaking so badly from exhaustion and excitement that I could hardly hold my camera to take a picture (which is why it's so blurry!) When I was picking up my coal to drop into my tinder

Very blurry photo of my very first bowdrill coal, April 2005, California.

bundle, I almost shook the whole thing off the coal-catcher. Looking back, I now realize that stopping to take that photo was probably what saved my coal in that moment. The time it took me to get out my camera and turn it on and take the photo gave my fragile coal enough time to coalesce and consolidate so that I didn't break it apart with my shaking. Funny how those things just work out sometimes!

Somehow I managed to get that magical little coal into my bundle of fuzzed-out jute string without destroying it, and I started to blow. It got redder and redder and redder, and so much smoke was coming out of the tinder that I started to choke when I breathed in. (Little tip: turn your body so the smoke is blowing AWAY from you, not straight into your face!) More red, more smoke, more red, more smoke, more red, more smoke, then suddenly, FIRE!!!! I had done it! I had made FIRE!

My very first tinder bundle blown up into flame.

That was over eleven years ago now, and I can still feel the excitement when I think back on that moment. For we humans, fire is life. Without the ability to make fire we would never have become what we are today. We would never have survived. Fire is our kindred spirit, our magical brother, and our truest friend. It is forever out there, in the ether, always watching, always waiting and always ready to appear whenever the proper conditions are met.

Bowdrill is just one of the ways in which we can bring forth fire using friction, and it is usually the first one that most people today encounter. Making fire from nothing is an incredible, magical, and life-changing experience. It brings you closer to the most basic elements that make up our world. It brings you in contact with the most fundamental rules of the universe that govern our very existence. It creates a bridge between you and your most ancient ancestors; those amazingly ingenious relatives of ours who figured it all out for the very first time. Think about that for just a moment. Think about all the different ways there are to do this wrong, and marvel that hundreds of thousands of years ago, those people we too often think of as "ignorant stone age savages", against all the odds, discovered how to get it right. The Einstein's, the Newton's, the DaVinci's and Tesla's of *their* age, cracked the codes of the laws of physics and the Universe, and discovered how to make fire, using friction.

Today we take fire for granted. We flip a switch and fire gives us light in the form of a bulb. We turn a knob and fire cooks our food in the form of a stovetop burner. We push a button and fire heats our homes via a boiler or a furnace. Fire is everywhere. Fire touches everything. But through this simple act of "rubbing two sticks together" we, for a brief moment, can be the ones to touch fire.

Fire is not magic, but it is most definitely magical. It is my hope that, through this book, you too will be able to discover your own magical connection with our amazing brother, Fire.

કેન્ફેન્ફેન્

"Fire is our kindred spirit, our magical brother and our truest friend. Fire Is Life."

~ *About the Author* ~

Julie Martin has been practicing Primitive & Survival Skills full time for the past 11 years and teaching for the last five. She was raised on a farm in the Mennonite region of Southern Ontario, where wild edibles, organic gardening and traditional methods of food preservation were a regular part of her everyday life. A love of animals and of the outdoors was cemented into her from the start, as she spent her childhood wandering the woods and fields on the family farm. She began riding her brother's pony at the age of 4, and has had a dog for a constant companion since before she can even remember.

After 15 years of traveling, and pursuing a career as an actor/singer/writer in cities throughout Canada and the United States, a serious car accident caused Julie to re-evaluate how she wanted to spend her time on this earth and in this life.

Julie spent some time recovering from her accident in the deserts of Utah. Upon learning of her desire to be able to "Aragorn" a set of tracks they came upon, a friend suggested she find a place to go and learn this ancient skill, so Julie did. What originally began as a way of overcoming the trauma from her accident quickly developed into a life-changing passion into which she jumped head-first and has never looked back. Soon after, she took an internship, which led to full-time employment, at The Tracker School. After a year spent increasing efficiency, improving student relations, reorganizing the Tracker office, and running the School Store, Julie left Tracker behind and, together with Eddie Starnater, founded *Practical Primitive* in 2007.

While fascinated and humbled by all the skills of our ancestors, Julie's biggest passions have become fire, flintknapping and of course, plants. She continues to follow her strong and uncompromising vision to provide a place where people can receive hands-on instruction and experience as they discover just how amazing the natural world can be.

Julie has been interviewed in publications ranging from *Wilderness Way* to *The New York Times,* and featured in multiple television segments for local and network news programs, including *ABC World News Tonight.*

She works and lives in New Jersey with her amazing partner of eleven years, Eddie Starnater, and their ridiculously adorable dog, Boomer.

For additional information on making Fire-by-Friction, Survival, Bushcraft, Wild Plants, Tracking, Primitive Skills, Traditional Living and more, join us for one of our upcoming workshops and/or webinars.

To see all the Fire-making videos referenced in this book, check out our YouTube channel at <u>www.youtube.com/PracticalPrimitive</u>.

For more on our books, DVDs, workshops and online courses visit our website at **www.PracticalPrimitive.com**.

We hope you enjoyed the information presented and will practice it responsibly. As we always say, if you had fun and learned something please tell everyone you know, and if you didn't, please tell us so we can fix it. Now get out there, get to know Fire, Have Fun, and Be Well.

*Practical Primitive provides Hands-on Learning in
Primitive Skills, Traditional Living, Bushcraft
Self-Reliance & Wilderness Survival*

Small group, weekend workshops for Adults
Intensive Skills Programs / Virtual Instruction / Skills 2 You
www.practicalprimitive.com
info@practicalprimitive.com
www.facebook.com/practicalprimitive
908-637-8137

Made in the USA
Lexington, KY
18 May 2018